The Upstream Christian in a Down- stream World

Charles W. Dunn

This book is designed for your personal reading pleasure and profit. It is also designed for group study. A leader's guide with helps and hints for teachers and visual aids (Victor Multiuse Transparency Masters) is available from your local bookstore or from the publisher.

VICTOR

BOOKS a division of SP Publications, Inc.
WHEATON, ILLINOIS 60187

Offices also in
Whitby, Ontario, Canada
Amersham-on-the-Hill, Bucks, England

Fifth printing, 1983

Recommended Dewey Decimal Classification: 248.5
   Suggested Subject heading: Christian Life

Library of Congress Catalog Card Number: 79–65191
ISBN: 0–88207–789–9

© 1979 by SP Publications, Inc. All rights reserved
Printed in the United States of America

VICTOR BOOKS
A division of SP Publications, Inc.
P.O. Box 1825, Wheaton, Illinois 60187

To
Charlie, Joshua,
Teresa, and Maria,
that they may always
go upstream

Contents

Preface

Confronting culture rather than compromising with culture is the theme of *The Upstream Christian in a Downstream World*. Christianity's greatest moments, beginning with Jesus Christ and the early church, have always been while going upstream against the currents of culture.

The background and burden for this book derive from some 30 years of seeing gaps between profession and possession, promise and performance in Christian living. It is my hope that this book may in some way help Christians close the gaps.

Many pastors, Sunday School teachers, and other Christians have influenced my life since I trusted Jesus Christ as Lord and Saviour at the age of seven on April 15, 1948. Although I cannot thank them all here, I do wish to thank Hugh McCoy, H. I. Newell, Evelyn Davis, and Ruth Brumme. To my mother is due special thanks, because this book taps but a small portion of her reservoir of wisdom. My wife, Carol, and our four children have immeasurably helped in providing examples and wisdom also.

To Jim Adair, who first asked me to write this book, and to those who edited it, I am deeply grateful.

Soli Deo Gloria,
Charles W. Dunn

"So likewise, whosoever he be of you that forsaketh not all that he hath, he cannot be My disciple."
Luke 14:33

1

Computing the Cost

Bombs rumbled like thunder. Antiaircraft explosions flashed like lightning. And I crouched fearfully in a trench. It was a dark and dreadful Tuesday night in 1969 at Uli Airport in Biafra, the name given the short-lived breakaway state in the eastern region of Nigeria, Africa.

In the trench, I awaited a rescue plane and prepared for the next bombing attack, while memories of four days and nights in the depths of Africa raced through my mind.

I shall long remember the mothers and small children going to the market in the dark, early hours of the morning. Market began and ended before daybreak to avoid the daily bombing attacks which had killed many innocent women and children in the marketplace.

I shall not soon forget the kwashiorkor clinics for children suffering from this severe form of protein deficiency. The jet black hair of the children had turned red and their stomachs were large and puffy. The little children, however, always had a friendly smile as they said, "Hi, welcome to Biafra."

I cannot erase the sight of a woman I met early one morning coming to a feeding center to obtain her one meal for the day. On her back was the last of five children. Starvation had claimed the other four. She had walked four miles that morning before daybreak to obtain one ball of cornmeal for herself and her child.

I shall not soon forget attending church early one Sunday

9

morning in the middle of Biafra's bush country. The church was packed to overflowing, and people were hanging in from the windows to participate in the service.

There was a commitment among the Biafran people that unified them in the face of adversity. Their spirit joined them in a common purpose. They were prepared to discipline their lives and sacrifice their material goods to achieve independence from the federal government of Nigeria. Except for the overwhelming military odds and the plague of starvation, they might have succeeded.

But they tragically miscalculated. They counted on a short war which they hoped to win with a blitzkrieg attack against the federal forces. After a few early successes it fizzled. They anticipated support from many nations, but only a handful ever gave them any help. They failed to provide for lack of protein supply after access to sea trade was cut off.

I escaped with my life from Biafra, but many others were not so fortunate.

Computing the Cost

Would Biafra's Ibo tribe people have undertaken their disastrous campaign if they had accurately calculated the cost? It's very doubtful. Yet people every day all over the world miscalculate the cost of following Jesus Christ. Jesus warned us against the danger. Great throngs of people were following Jesus when He spoke these fateful words. Clearly, He did not want anyone to miscalculate the cost of living the Christian life.

And there went great multitudes with Him; and He turned, and said unto them, "If any man come to Me, and hate not his father, and mother, and wife, and children, and brethren, and sisters, yea, and his own life also, he cannot be My disciple. And whosoever doth not bear his cross, and come after Me, cannot be My disciple.

"For which of you, intending to build a tower, sitteth not down first, and counteth the cost, whether he have sufficient to finish it? Lest haply, after he hath laid the foundation, and is not able to finish it, all that behold it begin to mock him, saying, 'This man began to build, and was not able to finish.'

"Or what king, going to make war against another king, sitteth not down first, and consulteth whether he be able with ten thousand to meet him that cometh against him with twenty thousand? Or else, while the other is yet a great way off, he sendeth an ambassage, and desireth conditions of peace. So likewise, whosoever he be of you that forsaketh not all that he hath, he cannot be My disciple.

"Salt is good: but if the salt have lost his savor, wherewith shall it be seasoned? It is neither fit for the land, nor yet for the dunghill; but men cast it out. He that hath ears to hear, let him hear" (Luke 14:25-35).

Three times in this passage Jesus says there are certain types of people who "cannot be My disciple."

First, if a person places family ahead of Jesus Christ, he cannot be Jesus' disciple. A believer once titled his book *I Am Third*—to indicate the place that Jesus and others have in his life.

Second, if a person does not take up his cross, he cannot be Jesus' disciple. Accepting one's cross means a person must be willing to walk the pathway Jesus walked. Theologian J. C. Ryle said: "An easy Christianity without a cross will prove in the end a useless Christianity without a crown." Paul told what it meant for him in his Letter to the Philippians:

But what things were gain to me, those I counted loss for Christ. Yea doubtless, and I count all things but loss for the excellency of the knowledge of Christ Jesus my Lord; for whom I have suffered the loss of all things, and do count them but dung, that I may win Christ, and be found in Him, not having mine own righteousness, which is of the law, but that which is through the faith of Christ, the righteousness which is of God by faith; that I may know Him, and the power of His resurrection, and the fellowship of His sufferings, being made conformable unto His death; if by any means I might attain unto the resurrection of the dead (3:7-11).

Third, if a person does not forsake everything that he has, he cannot be Jesus' disciple. The rich young ruler was unwilling to forsake his money (Mark 10:17-23). Pilate was unwilling to risk his popularity with the people by ruling honestly in Jesus' behalf (Luke 23). King Agrippa was unwilling to endanger his position by trusting Jesus Christ (Acts 26). Pecuniary concerns, public opinion, and position—three great fears—prevented these men from following Jesus Christ. "The fear of man bringeth a snare; but whoso putteth his trust in the Lord shall be safe" (Prov. 29:25). When we fear what may happen to our money, our standing with others, or our position, we cannot be Christ's disciples.

Cross of the Three Ts

The cross of the three Ts means that our *time*, our *talent*, and our *treasure*, belong to Jesus Christ. They must all be used for Him all of the time.

Paul reiterated this truth clearly: "I beseech you therefore, brethren, by the mercies of God, that ye present your bodies a living sacrifice, holy, acceptable unto God, which is your reasonable service. And be not conformed to this world, but be ye transformed by the renewing of your mind, that you may prove what is that good, and acceptable, and perfect will of God" (Rom. 12:1-2).

Time. How well we use our time will be judged by God. "So then every one of us shall give account of himself to God" (Rom. 14:12). Jesus revealed: "Every idle word that men shall speak, they shall give account thereof in the day of judgment" (Matt. 12:36). The writer of Ecclesiastes warned young people: "Rejoice, O young man, in thy youth; and let thy heart cheer thee in the days of thy youth, and walk in the ways of thine heart, and in the sight of thine eyes; but know thou, that for all these things God will bring thee into judgment" (Ecc. 11:9).

One of the ways to check on your time is to ask what you do with the obviously idle moments—sitting in a doctor's office, waiting at a traffic light, riding on a bus or a train, walking to or from work or school. I have learned to use this time for Scripture memorizing by always carrying a packet of Bible verse cards to fill idle moments.

Psychologists tell us that approximately 10,000 thoughts go through our minds each day. The Christian's goal should be to consolidate these thoughts on godly concerns, such as Scripture memory and prayer. My son, Charlie, during his first grade, memorized about 30 verses while I drove him to school each morning. That time edified both his mind and his spirit.

Talent. In the parable of the talents, Jesus taught that we are to invest our talents to earn dividends for the kingdom of God. At His return He will see how well we have invested our talents.

A fellow professor is particularly gifted in ministering to the needs of others, helping and showing mercy. Constantly he has his eye on someone who needs help. I have seen him in the coldest part of winter check on elderly people to be sure they have adequate fuel for heat, and ample food. This professor knows how God has gifted him, and he uses those talents wisely.

Not only does this ministry bring glory to God, but it also builds and maintains the body of Christ, the church. Paul emphasized the importance of our gifts to the church. "Now concerning spiritual gifts, brethren, I would not have you ignorant" (1 Cor. 12:1). If we are ignorant of our spiritual gifts, the body of Christ suffers, because there is a missing link. Should my professor friend neglect to invest his talents, the people who need his ministry would suffer.

Treasure. Jesus commended the widow who gave her two mites, because she gave her all. And He told His disciples, "Give, and it shall be given unto you; good measure, pressed down, and shaken together, and running over" (Luke 6:38). It is as we give that we receive.

About 4:30 one Monday morning, something awakened me. My mind quickly turned to a Nigerian student who had come to the United States, without financial assistance, to seek a medical education that he might return to his village and minister to his people. A few months before, he had come to Clemson

University, during the coldest winter in modern history, without a winter coat and with very few clothes. I soon learned that his prayer life was deeper than that of anyone else I knew. That morning God led me to call him to my office so I could give him $500. I did not have $500, and I knew that a bank loan would be the only way I could give him the money. He did not have a job, and without $500 he would not have been able to attend summer school. Within a week after giving my friend the $500, I was handed a check from another person for $450. Every time I have given as Christ has commanded, He has not failed to meet my needs and more. I concluded that the Lord thought I could afford the other $50.

While praying to find a foreign missionary for my wife and me to support, I met a young man, with a wife and three children, who desired to serve God in Spanish-speaking countries, particularly in Puerto Rico, where he had been born. I was unaware that no person or church had at that time committed any money to him. I shared the matter with my wife, and we knew that God wanted us to support this family. Our $50 per month became their first income. Since then they have visited us in our home several times. Now our children know their children well and we feel close to a missionary family solidly established in Puerto Rico. A small gift has led to a personal stake in presenting Christ to Puerto Rico.

Truthfully, we have received far more in blessings from our gifts to the Nigerian student and the missionary family than we have ever given, but that is according to God's promise.

Marks of the "Christian Atheist"

Many people who claim to be Christians have commitments that fall far short of living by "the cross of the three Ts." An atheist does not believe there is a God; a "Christian atheist" believes in God but lives as though His demands and promises are not important. There are several ways to recognize a "Christian atheist."

Selfishness. Many people attend church every time the church door opens but seem more concerned about themselves and their advancement than about Christ and the advancement of the kingdom of God. This type of person does not have the time to witness, to visit the sick, to host a Bible study or prayer meeting in his home, or to give sacrificially to those in need. He is like those who passed by the injured and robbed man on the Jericho Road. Only the Good Samaritan finally took the time to stop, reach down, bandage the wounds, carry the man to safety, and pay for his care. The excuses of passersby were probably nicely worded: "I'm in a hurry to attend a very important meeting;" "But what if the robbers should return and harm both of us?" "I need to get professional help for this person;" "We pay taxes to help people in trouble." As Solomon wrote: "The backslider in heart shall be filled with his own ways" (Prov. 14:14).

One night in Washington, D.C., my wife and I were passing by the Department of Health, Education, and Welfare during the peak of the "black power movement." A car was stalled there, and I stopped to help. Even though the burly black man with a wrench in his hand did not need my help, he discovered that at least one white man cared enough to stop in a time of racial unrest. I find that if I stop to ponder performing a good deed, many excuses pop into my mind about why I cannot or should not. When I fail to do God's will, it's often because I have delayed action to think about it—to find some excuse.

Indifference. Jesus said: "And because iniquity shall abound, the love of many shall wax cold" (Matt. 24:12). A young husband and father often used to promise that he would attend an early morning Bible study and prayer meeting, assuring me that he really wanted to come. He would attend a time or two and then stop coming. If I encouraged him, he attended again for another time or two. When the church had a revival meeting, he always seemed to get "revived," being one of the first persons to walk the aisle. But his commitment never seemed to stick. He was unwilling to repent (turn from) all of his sin; when he came down from the mountaintop of a Christian experience into the valley of the world, his desire to follow his commitment "waxed cold."

Dr. Bob Jones, Sr., the well-known evangelist and college president of yesteryear, remarked that "the greatest ability is dependability." Perhaps you have met the type of person who is afraid to say No to people. This type of person says he will be at prayer meeting or go witnessing. He agrees because he wants to please everyone, but no one can depend on him. Somehow he never makes it to the prayer meeting or has the time for personal evangelism. In reality, he is indifferent to the things he should do but he wants to create the impression that he is seriously interested. Most of the discipleship sessions I have with men are at 6:30 A.M., because I want to find out if they are really committed and dependable. If a man is dependable at 6:30 A.M., I can be pretty sure he will be dependable at other times.

Bondage to form. Paul warned Timothy about people who have a form of godliness, but who deny the power thereof. "From such turn away" (2 Tim. 3:5). Though I have been in denominational churches most of my life, I've found that sometimes these churches strive to convert people to their own forms of denominationalism—rather than striving to bring people to Jesus Christ. Of course, independents can make the same mistake. The religious organization of Jesus' day was in bondage to its form and He condemned it. Whenever any church is more concerned about the form than the function of the church, it risks the same judgment. Paul also spoke of this bondage to form in Galatians 4:9-10: "But now, after that you have known God, or rather are known of God, how turn ye again to the weak and beggarly elements, whereunto ye desire again to be in bondage? You observe days, and months, and times and years."

Some churches refuse to financially support their own members as missionaries because they are not in denominational missions. A church voted not to support one of its own deacons who was called to mission work outside of denominational sponsorship; yet he was one of the strongest Christians in the church.

Lack of spiritual enthusiasm. Writing to the church at Ephesus, John said: "Nevertheless I have somewhat against thee, because thou hast left thy first love" (Rev. 2:4). When Christians lose their first love of the Lord Jesus Christ, they lose their joy of witnessing. It is encouraging to see new Christians who enjoy witnessing and being in fellowship with other Christians. But how discouraging to see a Christian's enthusiasm fade away with time as his love for the Lord Jesus Christ becomes cold.

One of the most dramatic testimonies I ever heard was given by a man who had been an alcoholic and the owner of several taverns. He was converted on a Sunday morning, and on Monday morning he began to dispose of his businesses. For several years it seemed as if he could not do enough for the Lord. Then a spiritual hardening of the arteries set in. His new business seemed to require more time and he no longer witnessed and fellowshipped with Christians as before. He still attended church, but the glow of his first love had vanished. He seemed to be just going through the motions of being a Christian.

A look at his life showed a major cause of the spiritual aloofness. During the period of his intense spiritual interest he never learned to dig deeply into God's Word; as a result, his knowledge of the Bible remained shallow. Bible study is like soil tilling: it must be conducted regularly and deeply to produce crops.

Another young man, raised in a Christian home and good church, went to seminary where his spiritual enthusiasm waned. Investigation showed the professors undermined his faith in the Bible and eroded the foundation of his spiritual life. I have seen this occur many times, even to students who are fully aware that some of their professors do not uphold the authority of Scripture.

The foundation of spiritual enthusiasm is God's Word, and we should remove ourselves from faith-destroying places or situations, such as seminaries propagating a defective view of Scripture, in order to preserve our first love.

"The Lord helps those who help themselves?" When I was teaching a Sunday School class, two businessmen in insurance and real estate quoted what they thought was in Scripture: "The Lord helps those who help themselves." Of course, if that is

really true then God is obliged to assist even the Mafia. My response was to quote several verses about waiting on God, such as Psalm 27:14 and Isaiah 40:31, and several on faith, such as Romans 4:20-21. We find beautiful illustrations from life of God's faithfulness to those who faithfully follow Him in obedience.

• Missionaries with a certain mission organization were directed to wait upon God for financial support. Today that group has one of the largest Protestant missionary organizations.

• Abraham's example gives adequate instruction about God's helping us. Abraham "staggered not at the promise of God through unbelief; but was strong in faith, giving glory to God; and being fully persuaded that, what He had promised, He was able also to perform" (Rom. 4:20-21).

Bite the bullet. In a meeting of church leaders concerned about church finances, one man said: "Well, the money just isn't here. We'll just have to bite the bullet." Sadly, this view was widespread throughout the church. Its offering to missions—local and foreign—was shameful. Its building was in poor condition. They were constantly "biting the bullet" rather than launching out by faith to attempt great things for God. They forgot that God's resources are available to support His work. The psalmist said that God owns the cattle on a thousand hills (Ps. 50:10). We are told that if God calls us to do something, He will be faithful to provide (1 Thes. 5:24). The godly person never bites the bullets.

Chock-full of excuses. "Nobody's perfect." "He's such a nice person." "She's only mixed-up." "Everybody has to do his own thing." These are excuses of persons trying to rationalize a way of life contrary to the will of God. Humanly, a person may be nice, but from heaven's viewpoint, no one is really OK short of knowing Jesus Christ as personal Lord and Saviour. Humanly, doing your own thing is understandable, but divinely, doing your own thing is fatal. It is contrary to doing God's will. Humanly, nobody's perfect; but divinely, God demands perfection—and gives it through the Lord Jesus Christ.

Trifling with God

The practice of the "Christian atheist" must be seriously weighed against Scripture, because God says "examine yourselves whether ye be in the faith" (2 Cor. 13:5). Consider God's warnings to those whose works do not back up their words.

"Blessed are the pure in heart; for they shall see God. . . . Blessed are they which are persecuted for righteousness' sake; for theirs is the kingdom of heaven" (Matt. 5:8, 10).

"Whosoever therefore shall be ashamed of Me . . . of him also shall the Son of Man be ashamed, when He cometh in the glory of His Father with the holy angels" (Mark 8:38).

"No man, having put his hand to the plow, and looking back, is fit for the kingdom of God" (Luke 9:62).

"Every branch in Me that beareth not fruit He taketh away. . . . If a man abide not in Me, he is cast . . . into the fire and . . . burned" (John 15:2, 6).

"For if you live after the flesh, you shall die" (Rom. 8:13).

"Neither the sexually immoral nor idolaters nor adulterers nor male prostitutes nor homosexual offenders nor thieves nor the greedy nor drunkards nor slanderers nor swindlers will inherit the kingdom of God" (1 Cor. 6:9-10, NIV).

"No whoremonger, nor unclean person, nor covetous man, who is an idolater, hath any inheritance in the kingdom of Christ and of God" (Eph. 5:5).

"For it is impossible for those who were once enlightened, and have tasted of the heavenly gift, and were made partakers of the Holy Ghost, and have tasted the good word of God, and the powers of the world to come, if they shall fall away, to renew them again unto repentance; seeing they crucify to themselves the Son of God afresh, and put Him to an open shame" (Heb. 6:4-6).

"For if we sin willfully after that we have received the knowledge of the truth, there remaineth no more sacrifice for sins, but a certain fearful looking for of judgment and fiery indignation, which shall devour the adversaries" (Heb. 10:26-27).

"Now the just shall live by faith; but if any man draw back, My soul shall have no pleasure in him" (Heb. 10:38).

"Follow peace with all men, and holiness, without which no man shall see the Lord" (Heb. 12:14).

"And if the righteous scarcely be saved, where shall the ungodly and the sinner appear?" (1 Peter 4:18).

". . . give diligence to make your calling and election sure" (2 Peter 1:10).

"So then because thou art lukewarm, and neither cold nor hot, I will spew thee out of My mouth" (Rev. 3:16).

"Blessed are they that do His commandments, that they may have right to the tree of life, and may enter in through the gates into the city" (Rev. 22:14).

Vows

"When thou vowest a vow unto God, defer not to pay it; for He hath no pleasure in fools" (Ecc. 5:4). To commit oneself to Jesus Christ as Lord and Saviour is to take the most serious of vows. How foolish it is to make a profession of trusting Jesus Christ but to continue trusting oneself. Jeremiah 17:5-8 gives some evidence of God's thinking on this matter.

Thus saith the Lord: "Cursed be the man that trusteth in man, and maketh flesh his arm, and whose heart departeth from the Lord. For he shall be like the heat in the desert, and shall not see when good cometh; but shall inhabit the parched places in the wilderness, in a salt land and not inhabited. Blessed is the man that trusteth in the Lord, and whose hope the Lord is. For he shall be as a tree planted by the waters, and that spreadeth out her roots by the river, and shall not see when heat cometh, but her leaf shall be green; and shall not be careful in the year of drought, neither shall cease from yielding fruit."

Poignantly putting this passage in contemporary perspective, A. W. Tozer said, in *Of God and Men*,

Evangelicalism as we know it today . . . *does* produce some real Christians. . . . But the spiritual climate into which many modern Christians are born does not make for vigorous spiritual growth. Indeed, the whole evangelical world is to a large extent unfavorable to healthy Christianity. And I am not thinking of modernism either. I mean rather the Bible-believing crowd that bears the name of orthodoxy. . . .

We are making converts to an effete type of Christianity that bears little resemblance to that of the New Testament. The average so-called Bible Christian in our times is but a wretched parody of true sainthood. Yet we put millions of dollars behind movements to perpetuate this degenerate form of religion, and attack the man who dares challenge the wisdom of it (*Of God and Men.* Christian Publications, 1960, pp. 12-13).

"That He would grant unto us, that we being delivered out of the hand of our enemies might serve Him without fear, in holiness and righteousness before Him, all the days of our life."

Luke 1:74-75

2

The Diamond Dimensions of Discipleship

Diamonds are the hardest natural substance known. They are also the most popular gem, and in gemstone symbolism represent steadfast love. A rough drawing of a diamond commonly contains four sides, which we may liken to four dimensions of the Christian disciple: *dependence, durability, delightfulness,* and *diffusion.*

A diamond *depends* upon tremendous heat and pressure for its development, an expert cutting for its high value, and light for displaying its beauty. A diamond is so *durable* it cuts steel. And it is *delightful* to look at because it receives and then *diffuses* light into the brilliant colors of the spectrum. In the Bible, John the Baptist's life illustrates these diamond dimensions of discipleship.

Dependence

Just as the diamond is dependent upon certain conditions for its development, on its cut and polish for its value, and on light to show its beauty, so too the Christian has similar dependencies.

A Christian has a place of development. For John the Baptist, we note that his parents were spiritually influential, "walking in all the commandments and ordinances of the Lord blameless" (Luke 1:6). Clearly the prophecy and call of God was upon John's life (Luke 1:14-17, 76-79). Verse 15 foretold: "He shall be great in the sight of the Lord, and shall drink neither wine nor strong drink; and he shall be filled with the Holy Ghost, even from his mother's womb.'' Rigorous living provided the finishing touches on the prophet. ''And the child grew, and waxed strong in spirit, and was in the deserts till the day of his showing unto Israel'' (Luke 1:80).

In a sense, the head of the household is the spiritual foreman of a development mine. Accordingly, he must take seriously God's laws. ''And thou shalt teach them diligently unto thy children, and shalt talk of them when thou sittest in thine house, and when thou walkest by the way, and when thou liest down, and when thou risest up'' (Deut. 6:7). John the Baptist's parents followed this biblical precept.

As the father of four children, I have a special responsibility to manage their *spiritual development.* One way is to read Bible stories to them. Indeed, they will hardly go to bed without having Christian books read to them. Charlie, my oldest, had been through many story books by the time he was seven, and some he had literally memorized. Joshua, at the age of four, suggested he begin a Scripture memory program. He also asked that we read a portion of Scripture before each meal and that I ask questions about the passage. First, we went through all the Psalms and then all of Proverbs. All of the children, including three-year-old Teresa, begged me to do this. Many times their mealtime prayers reflect what we have just read from the Bible. My oldest son began memorizing Scripture at a very early age and had memorized nearly 100 verses by age eight.

The Christian also depends upon *character* as a gauge of his value to God. God crafts our lives to produce a holy character. In Zacharias' prophecy about John the Baptist, he said God's purpose is that we ''serve Him without fear, in holiness and righteousness before Him, all the days of our life'' (Luke 1:74-75). Specifically, God wants pure lives that reveal the glory of their Maker in the grace and splendor of their polished traits.

The best diamonds are cut to maximize the reflection and refraction of light upon them. A ''flawless'' diamond cut to proper specifications gives off brilliant colors. In much the same way, a Christian whose character is refined and purified gives off a radiance that exalts the Master of his life.

One of the men I have discipled had a harsh countenance from frequenting bars and avoiding his responsibilities as husband and father. An amazing transformation took place in his countenance over the first 12 weeks while he was being taught how to grow as a Christian. The once coarse look became a contented face that radiated the joy of the Lord.

Paul wrote, "You are not your own, . . . you are bought with a price; therefore glorify God in your body" (1 Cor. 6:19-20). This verse indicates the high value placed on us by God, and our responsibility to shine for him with His own beauty.

Durability

In the diamond's atomic structure, each carbon atom is linked to four equidistant neighbors, creating a very solid and durable substance useful for both esthetic and industrial purposes. The word diamond came from the Greek word *adamas*, meaning "invincible," and the Roman poet Manilius applied it to diamonds in A.D. 16. The word *adamantine* now refers to a diamond's hard, brilliant lustre. Better quality diamonds are customarily used for adornment, while those of lesser quality are usually relegated to industrial uses. The owner of a diamond ring can depend upon it to retain its value and beauty, while the industrialist can depend upon his diamonds for durability. How are the qualities of durability and dependability developed in the Christian?

Looking again at John the Baptist, we see he had the discipline of *self-denial*. A man of plain dress—camel's hair, and plain food—locusts and wild honey, he lived apart from the comforts and standards of the world. Today's Christians have extraordinary pressures on them to live by worldly standards, and they can avoid succumbing to these pressures only by self-denial.

In our family, we had difficulty making Sunday truly the Lord's Day for worship in church, and for rest and relaxation at home. So many activities are now held on Sundays and many stores remain open. My wife, children, and I discussed the matter and decided that, based on Scripture, one day of the week should be set aside for strictly biblical purposes of worship, rest, and relaxation. Not, of course, that Sunday should find us living more holy lives, but if God found it important to work six days and then to rest the seventh, we should too. And if He found it important to tell the Israelites to labor six days and rest on the seventh day, we should too. The results of avoiding the worldly pressures to attend sports events, to shop, and go to parties have been most beneficial. Family life is developed, and the week days following always go better. Our children have come to understand and appreciate why God wants us to set aside one day like this for Him.

In our family we also had the typical television problem. I would come home from work and find the children watching TV with hardly a sign of recognition that their father had arrived. I knew that I was guilty of the same neglect for the children when watching the news or a sports program. Here again, we applied self-discipline and denial as a family, and though the television set remains in the same place, it is rarely turned on any more. When we returned a Neilson rating card recently, it showed we hadn't watched any programs. As a result, our family communicates more and we are a happier family.

God has used many individuals who were willing to deny and control their desires so they would be more durable and dependable. John Wesley, after preaching, traveling, and writing for 50 years with great impact on the spiritual and social fabric of Britain, died a pauper. C. T. Studd gave away his large inheritance and pioneered missions on three continents. God does not ask all of us to be like John the Baptist, but He is ready to profusely bless individuals who will, like John, practice self-denial for His sake.

The solid character of John the Baptist is also reflected in his *courage* amidst difficult circumstances. Jesus said John was a "burning and a shining light" (John 5:35). Sometimes that light was searing. "O generation of vipers, who hath warned you to flee from the wrath to come?'' (Luke 3:7) To those who were grossly unfruitful in their spiritual responsibilities, he warned, ''And now also the axe is laid unto the root of the trees; every tree therefore which bringeth not forth good fruit is hewn down, and cast into the fire'' (Luke 3:9).

John's bold witness led to his death when he denounced King Herod's marriage as unscriptural. Herein he demonstrated courage unto death, an important characteristic of Christians who face persecution, as noted in Revelation 12:11: ''And they overcame him by the blood of the Lamb, and by the word of their testimony; and they loved not their lives unto death.''

There were many times when John the Baptist could have compromised his mission, but he had a cutting message to deliver. The Christian witness today must sometimes cut before it can heal, because it is the message of Christ Himself to a sin-infested world. Like John the Baptist, we can declare: ''Prepare you the way of the Lord, make His paths straight. Every valley shall be filled, and every mountain and hill shall be brought low; and the crooked shall be made straight, and the rough ways shall be made smooth; and all flesh shall see the salvation of God'' (Luke 3:4-6).

A student in my college Sunday School class who had been a Christian leader on campus decided to go to the mission field. I had doubts about his durability because he had never left home, even to attend college, and had lived a sheltered life in the country's Bible Belt. The Christian organization he joined did not assign him overseas, but rather to a northeastern state. Even there, the young man did not last three months because he had not developed a diamondlike durability. Cold weather and calloused students were too harsh for an unproven, uncut diamond in the rough.

By virtue of its durability, a diamond has *value that increases* with age and can be passed on to others. The diamond I gave my wife is now worth several times more than I paid for it, and someday she will pass it along to a grateful daughter. As Christ's disciples, we are to possess a high value that increases with experience and attainment which can be shared profitably with others. Consider Jesus' words about John's value. "There hath not risen a greater than John the Baptist" (Matt. 11:11). By decreasing in the eyes of the world, John increased in value to God, and the characteristics of his life are written in Scripture to be passed along to our lives.

My brother did not become a Christian until 50 years of age, and he died in his early 60s. As I sat in the church funeral service, which overflowed with many non-Christians, I thought about how his life increased in value even in death because the Good News of Jesus Christ was preached at his funeral. Many times I ask myself if I am becoming more valuable to God with the passing of time.

Delightfulness

Who does not appreciate a diamond? Its beauty is irresistible. A quality diamond is transparent and flawless. Christians should also be transparent and holy so that Christ can be seen through their lives. A flawed diamond has uncrystallized carbon in it, lacking transparency and purity. Several areas in the Christian life are important if we are to have the diamondlike quality of holiness in our lives.

Thought Life. "Finally, brethren, whatsoever things are true, whatsoever things are honest, whatsoever things are just, whatsoever things are pure, whatsoever things are lovely, whatsoever things are of good report; if there be any virtue, and if there be any praise, think on these things" (Phil. 4:8).

Heart. "Keep thy heart with all diligence; for out of it are the issues of life" (Prov. 4:23).

Body. "What? know ye not that your body is the temple of the Holy Ghost which is in you, which ye have of God, and ye are not your own?" (1 Cor. 6:19)

Speech. "Let no corrupt communication proceed out of your mouth, but that which is good to the use of edifying, that it may minister grace unto the hearers" (Eph. 4:29).

A diamond does not require flashy settings to manifest its

beauty. There is an elegance which is sullied by gaudy accoutrements. Just so, a Christian's attractiveness resides in his character, not in conspicuous adornment. The radiance of Christ can be obscured by ostentatious display of our clothes or make-up.

It is important to note the related characteristic of humility. Modesty and humility went together in John the Baptist's life. Consider how John the Baptist referred to Jesus: *in power*, "One mightier than I"; *in preeminence*, "He . . . is above all"; *in precedence*, "He must increase but I must decrease" (Luke 3:16, John 3:30-31). The flaws of pride and jealousy were absent from John's life.

Diffusion

A diamond serves as a transmitter for light as well as a transformer of light. As a *transmitter*, a diamond receives and diffuses light; as a *transformer*, it changes the appearance of light into an array of hues. The high transmission-transformation sets diamonds afire by diffusing white light into its component colors.

We Christians are to receive and diffuse the light of God just as Jesus and as Paul did. "For even the Son of Man came not to be ministered unto, but to minister, and to give His life a ransom for many" (Mark 10:45). "For we preach not ourselves, but Christ Jesus the Lord, and ourselves your servants for Jesus' sake" (2 Cor. 4:5).

John the Baptist demonstrated the diamond quality of diffusion in his message: "Prepare ye the way of the Lord." We who have received the Light, Jesus, are channels for transmission to others. We portray in living colors the Light that dispels the darkness of the world. The Light we reflect brightens the way of the Lord into darkened hearts.

The best diamonds are expertly cut to increase the brilliance of the light diffused from them. Diamond cutting follows five steps that can be compared to the development of Christian character.

First, *the diamond is marked for removal of imperfections that detract from its value.* God has a comparable plan for our lives which will transform us into new persons. Paul described the change: "Therefore if any man be in Christ, he is a new creature; old things are passed away; behold, all things are become new" (2 Cor. 5:17). The Greek word for "are become" really means *are becoming*—that is, God's plan is to perfect us throughout our lives, conforming us more and more into the image of His perfect Son.

Second and third, *a diamond's imperfections are removed by the processes of cleaving and sawing.* God's tools to remove our imperfections are chastening or disciplining, the teaching of His Word under the guidance of His Spirit, and the fellowship of Christians (Heb. 12:6-11; 2 Tim. 3:16; John 16:13; 1 John 1:3).

Fourth, *the diamond base is rounded into a cone shape by the process of girdling.* Similarly, God desires that all Christians possess certain basic characteristics. Some of these are virtue, knowledge, temperance, patience, godliness, brotherly kindness, and love so that we might be "partakers of the divine nature" (2 Peter 1:4-8).

Fifth, *through the process of faceting, a diamond is cut* to the proper number of facets to most brilliantly reflect the light spectrum. So too, each Christian has a unique gift or set of gifts to minister to other members of the church body or to proclaim the Gospel, all the while reflecting the glory of God.

One of our family baby-sitters has a radiant smile that only God bestows. We did not know her before she became a Christian, but a Christian friend who had known her for many years told us: "She is no longer the same person. She was one of the roughest and wildest teenagers I knew. It is a miracle that she has that radiant smile now." The joy we saw was part of the divine Light shining from her transparent character.

A Christian woman once came to my wife and me for counsel about her failing marriage. We urged her to let Jesus be seen through her life. Although her husband was evidently at fault, she had magnified the problems by responding in non-Christlike ways. Sometime later she reported that God was giving her the grace to be Christlike in her attitudes and, although her husband still showed the same negative attitudes, she was serene and had regained hope that the beauty and lustre of her marriage would return. God was using marriage disharmony to develop diamond dimensions of discipleship in her life.

"See then that you walk circumspectly, not as fools, but as wise, redeeming the time, because the days are evil. Wherefore, be ye not unwise, but understanding what the will of the Lord is."

Ephesians 5:15-17

3

Knowing God's Will for Your Life

While beginning a chapel message at a Christian college, I asked those to stand who had ever had difficulty discerning the will of God for their lives. Immediately, everyone stood, including all the faculty, but seniors were first on their feet.

Whether there is a will of God that can be found always arouses great interest. At least three views about discerning the will of God exist. First, atheists like Bertrand Russell and Jean Paul Sartre argue there is no will of God to be discerned. Russell contended that we are but accidental collections of molecules, and Sartre says that the world we live in is closed to external or divine action.

Second are those, including many professing Christians, who think the will of God is an enigma, wrapped in a mystery, and shrouded in a puzzle. For these people, the will of God is mysterious and vague, and at best only accidentally or academically determined. To them, it is not very personal or specific in its application to each individual.

Third are the Christians who believe that God has a specific will for every person and He is ready to reveal it at the right time. For these persons, God cares about every aspect of one's life, as described in Psalm 139.

It is pointless to argue with atheists about God's plan or with those who do not believe God reveals His will or plan in the Bible. But we who trust God's revelation can discover a great

deal about the will of God in His Word. In searching the Scriptures, our questions are:
Does God truly have a plan for my life?
Are there prerequisites for knowing God's will?
What negative pitfalls must I avoid?
What positive principles guide my progress?

Does God Have a Plan for My Life?

If we examine the universe we find it to be very orderly. Planets move in a regular orbit. Plants grow according to botanical principles. Weather conditions develop according to atmospheric laws. The Creator of such a universe must Himself be orderly, with precise purposes for His created things.

It is logical to assume the God who carefully planned the physical universe has a definite purpose and function for the humans who inhabit it. Isaiah wrote: "I will say to the north, Give up; and to the south, Keep not back; bring My sons from far, and My daughters from the ends of the earth; even every one that is called by My name: for I have created him for My glory, I have formed him; yea, I have made him" (Isa. 43:6-7).

So the general purpose for God's people, according to the Bible, is to bring glory to God. The Bible further teaches that God has a specific purpose and function for each person who follows Him: "I will instruct thee and teach thee in the way which thou shalt go; I will guide thee with Mine eye" (Ps. 32:8). He told Isaiah: "I am the Lord thy God which teacheth thee to profit, which leadeth thee by the way that thou shouldest go" (Isa. 48:17).

These are but two of many Scriptures indicating that God has a will or plan for each life. Jesus said that the very hairs of our heads are numbered, that since God looks out for the sparrow that falls He will certainly look out for us, and that He who clothes the lilies of the field in splendor will surely care for us (Matt. 6:25-32).

Elsewhere throughout Scripture we are surrounded by specific divine plans at work: David, the shepherd boy, who became king;

Elisha, the farmer behind the plow, who became a great prophet; Nehemiah, the king's cupbearer, who became the restorer of Jerusalem; and childless Hannah, who gave birth to the great judge Samuel.

The prophet Jeremiah was informed by God: "Before I formed thee in the belly I knew thee; and before thou camest forth out of the womb I sanctified thee, and I ordained thee a prophet unto the nations" (Jer. 1:5).

Joseph told his brothers that God had ordained that he be sold into slavery so that he could rise to power in Egypt and help save the Hebrews from famine (Gen. 45:5).

Jesus said confidently: "To this end was I born, and for this cause came I into the world" (John 18:37).

For even the wicked and the ungodly, God appears to have a purpose. God through Moses said to the wicked Pharaoh: "But I have raised you up for this very purpose, that I might show you My power and that My name might be proclaimed in all the earth" (Ex. 9:16, NIV).

Over and over, the Bible shows the will of God at work in the lives of men and women. If you believe the Bible, you must believe in the will of God working in the details of people's lives.

Knowing God's Will: Three Prerequisites

A worried student came into my office one afternoon and voiced his concern about being admitted to graduate school. With a highly respected lawyer as a father, this young man wanted to take over his father's law practice following a year or two of graduate study in international relations and three years of law school. There were at least two reasons for the student's nervousness: he had a mediocre academic record, and he was reacting to parental pressures for success. I reflected that this student was way off the track—he simply was not gifted in academic pursuits. We talked about his situation, and I came to the two questions I always ask in counseling: "Do you know for certain that you have eternal life in heaven?" And, "Suppose you were to die tonight and stand before God, and He were to ask, 'Why should I let you into My heaven?' What would you say?''

To the first question, the student answered, "No." To the second, he said he would have much more to say about why he should be admitted to graduate school than to heaven. He realized that having the right answers to my questions was far more important than his gaining admission to graduate school.

I showed him from the Bible that it was God's will for him to be saved. "God . . . will have all men to be saved, and to come unto the knowledge of the truth" (1 Tim. 2:3-4). Then I showed him that God had a specific will or plan for his life. "Trust in the Lord with all thine heart; and lean not unto thine own understanding. In all thy ways acknowledge Him, and He shall direct thy paths" (Prov. 3:5-6).

Then I pointed out that before anyone can have God's guidance he must belong to God through trusting Jesus Christ as His Saviour and Lord. I asked if this way of salvation made sense to him, and he said, "Yes." Then I asked if he wanted to know God's will for his life, and he nodded. But when I asked if he were willing to confess and repent of his sins and to trust Jesus Christ, he said, "I want to think about it some more." I warned him from Scripture about the peril of putting off God's desire for Him, but he refused to take the first step.

This conversation illustrates the three prerequisites for knowing the will of God: first, being a child of God; second, obeying God; third, waiting on God.

The Bible tells us that "whatsoever is born of God overcometh the world; and this is the victory that overcometh the world, even our faith. Who is he that overcometh the world, but he that believeth that Jesus is the Son of God?" (1 John 5:4-5) To know and to do the will of God is to have victory in life. By refusing to put his faith in Jesus as the Son of God, the young man was disobeying God's will, and of course, he was not seeking God's guidance for his career. He left my office just as worried and nervous as when he entered.

On parting, I encouraged him from Isaiah 40:31: "But they

that wait upon the Lord shall renew their strength; they shall mount up with wings as eagles; they shall run, and not be weary; and they shall walk, and not faint."

Waiting on God is difficult even for Christians. Our culture conditions us to be self-reliant and make decisions quickly, but God says to wait upon His direction.

Scripture is filled with examples of those who failed to wait for the Lord's direction. Esau sold his birthright to Jacob for a bowl of porridge because he was in such a hurry to eat (Gen. 25:31). Saul lost his kingship because he would not wait for Samuel to offer the burnt offering (1 Sam. 13:8-13). Loss of something valuable is the cost of not waiting on God.

Abraham and his descendants have paid a high price for Abraham's failure to wait on God's timing to provide the promised heir through Sarah. Abraham got in a hurry and fathered Ishmael through Hagar, and the Arab nations that descended from Ishmael have been Israel's undying enemies.

One of the most difficult lessons I have had to learn as a Christian was to wait for God. I have had the tendency to push myself ahead rather than to wait for God to do with my life what He wants to do. God's words to Abraham were: "Get thee out of thy country and from thy kindred and from thy father's house unto the land that I will show thee. And I will make thee a great nation, and I will bless thee and make thy name great, and thou shalt be a blessing. And I will bless them that bless thee, and I will curse him that curseth thee. And in thee shall all the families of the earth be blessed" (Gen. 12:1-3).

Abraham first went out by faith into an unknown land. God may call us to take a step of faith, but we should not think that His promise to us will be fulfilled immediately upon taking the step of faith. Abraham did not live to see the total fulfillment of God's promise. Waiting for God's time is as much a part of faith as doing something for God.

A Christian student majoring in horticulture was uncertain about what to do after graduation, which was just one week away. He telephoned and asked to see me as soon as possible. I asked him to come immediately since he seemed in great distress. His mother wanted him to enroll in seminary upon graduation, and a Christian student organization wanted him to take staff training and join its ministry. He didn't know which to do, but he seemed certain that his horticulture training had been a waste of time.

I asked if there were any country in the world that did not need horticulturists. He said he didn't know of any. Then I asked if foreign mission service had ever entered his mind. He said, "No, but I would happily consider it." I reminded him that a Christian horticulturist might be more easily placed on the mission field than someone with a Bible college or seminary degree, especially in those countries closed to traditional mission work.

Then I suggested he go home to his parents and spend time with them out of respect and appreciation for their contributions to his life and education. I also suggested that he fast and pray as he waited upon the Lord to reveal His will for him. And I gave him the titles of missionary biographies that would challenge his thinking and increase his understanding of foreign missions. Finally, I asked that he study God's Word thoroughly on the matter of knowing God's will.

Family and peer pressures often make it hard to wait on the Lord to reveal His will. Some Christians hurry decisions in order to "save face." Either attending seminary or affiliating with the staff of the Christian organization would have been the "easy way out" for this student.

Several weeks later, I saw him working at a Christian retreat center. God still had not revealed the next step, but He had provided a job which allowed him to hear outstanding Christian teachers and to nurture his faith. He was no longer depressed and anxious. As he waited, God was revealing His will.

Seven Pitfalls

After years of Bible study and counseling people about finding God's will, I have learned seven pitfalls in determining the will of God.

- Do not second-guess God or yourself.
- Do not pattern your calling after another person's.
- Do not misunderstand God's character and desires.
- Do not take Bible verses out of context.
- Do not mistake "moonlight and roses" for God's will.
- Do not think a minister's or missionary's call is more important than anyone else's.
- Do not expect the revelation of God's will to produce a "liver shiver."

Second-guessing God and ourselves. Psalm 37:5 reads: "Commit thy way unto the Lord; trust also in Him; and He shall bring it to pass." Several principles can be derived from this verse which counsel against second-guessing.

Our covenant is with God. We accept His covenant with us. We do not decide what we are going to do for God, but rather we accept as our responsibility what He wants us to do for Him. There is no exception or option clause in God's contract with us. His way becomes our way.

Abraham "went out, not knowing whither he went" (Heb. 11:8). He was truly committing his way to God. Because he did, God brought to pass the great promises cited earlier, in Genesis 12:1-3. Abraham had many reasons to second-guess God, especially since he was rather well off right where he was.

At one point in my life while living in Washington, D.C., I chose to take a $10,000 salary cut in order to do God's will. I could have told God that I was very well off where I was: teaching a Sunday School class, sharing a weekly prayer meeting with fellow staff members of the U.S. Senate, and ministering in my church. Of course, I was also building the nice retirement income to which people on Capitol Hill are accustomed. I left to take a job that would terminate within 12 months. Today I am less secure financially than I was then, but a millionaire spiritually by comparison.

At other times in my life, especially during my teenage years, I could have told God: "I am from a poor family, and I had to wear rummage sale clothing as a boy. My parents never finished the eighth grade. I can't afford to do the things You want me to do.'' Fortunately, my mother taught me that God's favor and His people's grumbling do not mix. We read in Numbers 32:13 that ''the Lord's anger was kindled against Israel, and He made them wander in the wilderness 40 years, until all the generation that had done evil in the sight of the Lord was consumed.'' Their evil had been grumbling and rejection of God's will.

Young Christian men and women try to second-guess God regarding the choice of lifetime mates. One morning a student came into my office deeply concerned—not about the examination facing him the next hour and for which he had not studied—but about whether he should ask a certain girl for a date in two weeks. I asked him if God had called him to Clemson University to be the best Christian student he could be. When he answered affirmatively, I asked why he was more concerned about a possible date in two weeks than about the sure examination in one hour, especially since the girl had told him she did not want to date him again. This young man had not committed his way to the Lord, nor was he trusting the Lord for the woman God wanted him to marry.

I remember all the time I spent looking for a wife and how foolish God made me appear when He gave me a beautiful woman who was living 2,000 miles from where I was doing all that dating. I proposed on our second date, and she accepted on our third. Later I facetiously told her that she was not as much in tune with God's will as I. She, of course, had a different and perhaps a more accurate view. In God's time He brought us together and gave us both the assurance that we were His choice for each other.

Isn't the Christian life built primarily on personal relationships, first with God and then with fellow Christians? Neither my wife nor I have maintained much contact with the people we used to date, but we do maintain links with many of the Christian friends we had before marriage. Dating relationships are so transient, and they often sap us of spiritual fervor and commitment, as well as consuming so much time and energy.

Why not trust the Lord for one's marriage partner and stop spinning the dating wheels so much? Christians also second-guess God as they try to decide whether to live all-out for God. A bank vice-president, who graduated from a Christian college, told me he wanted to get on top in the banking profession before living all-out for God. He too had come from a relatively poor background, and he recognized that living all-out for God might endanger his chances for promotion in the bank. Was he living for God at all? Only he can answer that, but someday he will have to answer to God.

Knowing the will of God requires doing it, and a part of doing His perfect will is living all-out for Him right now. We must not second-guess God by telling Him there'll be time later to shift to full-time performance.

Copying another's calling. We must not pattern our calling after another's. Second Corinthians 10:12 reads: "For we dare not make ourselves of the number, or compare ourselves with some that commend themselves; but they measuring themselves by themselves, and comparing themselves among themselves, are not wise."

Comparison with another person leads to sin, either because we feel superior or inferior to him. No other human is God's standard for a Christian. I used to wonder if I taught or preached as effectively as other men, but God convinced me that He has uniquely gifted me and that my tasks are not patterned after anyone else's. How many men and women have missed God's plan because they have sought to pattern themselves after another's way!

Misunderstanding God's character. We must not misunderstand God's character: (1) by assuming that what we like cannot be God's will, (2) by thinking God's plan must be illogical, bizarre, or unpleasant, (3) by thinking previous violations of God's will prevent Him from using us now.

Many Scriptures speak forcefully with respect to each of these misunderstandings. For those who think that what we want cannot be God's will, the psalmist wrote: "Delight thyself also in the Lord; and He shall give thee the desires of thine heart" (Ps. 37:4). Paul wrote: "He that spared not His own Son, but delivered Him up for us all, how shall He not with Him also freely give us all things?" (Rom. 8:32) God is not an ogre who enjoys thwarting our desires. He wants to bless us, and sometimes that requires a change in our desires and in our attitudes.

The key to understanding these Scriptures is making sure that our desires are in accord with God's will. For many years, I sought a political career, and I had considerable success, although I was trying to brand my will as God's. Then I realized the truth of Isaiah 55:8-9: "For My thoughts are not your thoughts, neither are your ways My ways, saith the Lord. For as the heavens are higher than the earth, so are My ways higher than your ways, and My thoughts than your thoughts." My motive was wrong: I was seeking a political career to bring glory to myself and not to God. When I sincerely sought God's will, He revealed step-by-step His plan for my life, and it is far better than anything I had ever imagined.

Some think God's will must be bizarre or wild, or illogical, but Scripture and Christian experience teach the contrary. We need to remember, however, that: "the natural man receiveth not the things of the Spirit of God; for they are foolishness unto him; neither can he know them, because they are spiritually discerned" (1 Cor. 2:14). In God's mind, there is order, but that order may appear as disorder to natural man.

While on the faculty at the University of Illinois in 1972, I received two job offers. One was from the White House, asking if I would be interested in a staff position there. The other was from Clemson University, asking if I would be interested in heading their newly created Department of Political Science. Common sense pointed to the first. I didn't even know where Clemson University was, though I remembered it had been famous for great football teams. My life, at the age of 32, included four years of Capitol Hill staff experience in Washington, one year on a governor's staff, and one year with the Illinois

Constitutional Convention. It seemed only natural that a White House position would be the right place for me.

But God had a *supernatural* viewpoint. He led me to Clemson University, where I have since had two college textbooks published, taught a college Sunday School class touching 2,000 students' lives, and have had other unexpected outreaches. Was it bizarre or illogical to follow God's plan? Perhaps, in the fundamental decision to "go out, not knowing whither I went," but the result was poured-out blessings from heaven that I could not contain (Mal. 3:10).

Many people fear that a previous violation of God's will prevents God's present blessing. Scripturally, this is not so. King David committed adultery with Bathsheba and had her husband murdered, but God accepted David's prayer of repentance and confession and restored him (Ps. 51). We should note that although God forgave David, He did not wipe away the consequences of sin. The sin was removed, but the scar tissue remained, and David suffered severely. Peter denied Jesus three times, but God later used Peter to preach the Sermon at Pentecost when 3,000 persons were converted.

Verses out of context. We must not take Bible verses out of context. The classic illustration of a person finding God's will by opening his Bible and pointing to a verse is negatively instructive. According to the story, the person lighted on: "And Judas went out and hanged himself." Dissatisfied with this, he repeated the procedure and read: "Go and do thou likewise." Searching desperately a third time, he found: "What thou doest, do quickly."

I've seen people take one or a few verses out of context and present them as God's will for their lives. But Scripture is an integrated whole and must be dealt with accordingly. Our lives cannot declare the whole counsel of God unless they are built on the whole counsel.

A common mistake occurs when people disregard the Old Testament's moral law, because the New Testament says we no longer live under the Law, but under grace. The real meaning, of course, is "the law's *condemnation*." Jesus said He did not come to abolish the Law of the Old Testament, but fulfill or obey it (Matt. 5:17). We err grievously when we distort Scripture.

A teenage daughter of a deacon in another church was making attempts to talk with the dead, despite Scripture's clear admonition to avoid this sinful practice (Deut. 18:10-11). She had no knowledge of the Old Testament's law forbidding witchcraft.

Another common distortion concerns Scripture relating to Christian unity. For example, 1 Corinthians 1:10 reads: "Now I beseech you, brethren, by the name of our Lord Jesus Christ, that ye all speak the same thing, and that there be no divisions among you; but that you be perfectly joined together in the same mind and in the same judgment." Accordingly, some Christians call for unity even at the expense of truth.

But as the late B. H. Carroll, president of Southwestern Seminary, said: "It's better to have division over truth than unity around error." Scripture itself counsels that discipline be practiced in the church (1 Cor. 5), and for the sake of the Gospel witness, Christians should separate themselves from deviant and abnormal members. So division is more important than unity when "sound doctrine" is at stake.

While we do not have complete control of the uses to which our tithes and offerings are put, as individuals and church members, we have responsibility to give to causes and organizations which follow scriptural goals. Unfortunately, some churches allow their offerings to support colleges, seminaries, and mission works that teach false doctrine.

Moonlight and roses. We must not identify moonlight and roses with God's will for our lives. God has not promised us a rose garden in this life. "Whom the Lord loveth, He chasteneth, and scourgeth every son whom He receiveth" (Heb. 12:6). "Blessed are they which are persecuted for righteousness sake; for theirs is the kingdom of heaven" (Matt. 5:10). When things are easiest, watch out; you may be far removed from God's will. "But the God of all grace . . . after that you have suffered awhile, make you perfect, stablish, strengthen, settle you" (1 Peter 5:10).

While God has not promised us roses, He has promised us the peacefulness of a garden in our hearts. "Thou wilt keep him in perfect peace whose mind is stayed on Thee; because he trusteth in Thee" (Isa. 26:3). Jesus said: "Peace I leave with you, My peace I give to you; not as the world giveth, give I unto you. Let not your heart be troubled, neither let it be afraid" (John 14:27). Peace to the world means absence of conflict; to the Christian it is the peace of Jesus Christ in one's life amidst conflict. Jesus assured us: "These things I have spoken unto you, that in Me ye might have peace. In the world ye shall have tribulation; but be of good cheer; I have overcome the world" (John 16:33).

After being at Clemson University for two years, I was asked by the faculty committee of the College of Liberal Arts to deliver the annual lecture at the Honors and Awards Day Convocation. God informed me: "You are to give testimony to My Son, Jesus." Imagine giving testimony to Jesus Christ on a university campus before sociology, psychology, history, English, and music professors! Some walked out on me, and others would not speak to me for some time. Doing God's will was not a rose garden on that occasion.

I was also led of God to oppose the sale of beer in the student union building, and I wrote a five-page letter to the university president giving reasons why beer should not be sold there. That too, had repercussions.

The calling. We must not think a minister's or missionary's call is more important than any other Christian's call. For the present, God has called me to be a university professor just as He has called my pastor to minister to our congregation. We have both been set apart by God for the Gospel ministry. God has placed me where I am to reach people my pastor cannot reach. Both of us are an indispensable part of the body of Christ. Some of the best preaching and discipling I have ever experienced was from laymen. Romans 10:13–15 shows that every Christian has been called to proclaim the Gospel of Jesus Christ. "For whosoever shall call upon the name of the Lord shall be saved. How then shall they call on Him in whom they have not believed? And how shall they believe in Him of whom they have not heard? And how shall they hear without a preacher? And how shall they preach, except they be sent? As it is written, How beautiful are the feet of them that preach the Gospel of peace, and bring glad tidings of good things.''

The "liver-shiver." We must not think that God's revelations of His will to us should cause a "liver-shiver" reaction with goose bumps breaking out all over us. Remember that Satan can play tricks with our feelings, making us feel good while doing wrong. Paul explained: "And no marvel; for Satan himself is transformed into an angel of light" (2 Cor. 11:14).

One of my students, a Roman Catholic, had been following the teachings of an eastern guru for some time. One night he opened the Bible he had been given for high school graduation and saw that verse. He realized immediately that Satan had been working through the guru, appearing as an angel of truth and light. The youth's feelings had deceived him.

The Bible is written that we may *know reality*. First John 5:13 says: "These things have I written unto you that believe on the name of the Son of God; that you may know that you have eternal life, and that you may believe on the name of the Son of God." Paul said: "I know whom I have believed, and am persuaded that He is able to keep that which I have committed unto Him against that day" (2 Tim. 1:12).

Seven Positive Principles

Knowing God's will may entail looking at seven fundamental scriptural principles, or what I call the "seven Cs": (1) counsel of Christians, (2) commandments of God, (3) communion with God, (4) contentment, (5) circumstances, (6) conviction, and (7) careful thought.

One night in 1972, the phone rang after I had gone to bed. The caller was an insurance executive who had a major proposal: would I like to run for a seat in the Illinois legislature? As county political chairman, he was in a position to assist my candidacy. The prospect of a seat in the legislature where Abraham Lincoln once served fed a dream that I had long cherished.

I couldn't give an answer that night. I wanted my wife Carol to join me in praying for God's will in the matter. For three weeks we prayed, talked with political figures in the district, discussed the matter with Christians, and carefully thought about the pros and cons.

Circumstantially, it appeared as though I should run. I had grown up in the district, knew the political figures well, and had extensive experience in government. And the leading political official in the district was inviting me to run.

Why was it that at the end of three weeks I said to my wife, "We're not to run for that office"?

Counsel of Christians. Christians were divided in their counsel to me. Some were enthusiastic about my running. Others thought that God could better use my talents elsewhere. Proverbs 15:22 reads: "Without counsel purposes are disappointed; but in the multitude of counselors they are established." The fact that some Christians did not uniformly counsel me to run made me pause.

Commandments of God. A Christian president of a bank, following prayer, wrote me an unsolicited letter in which he quoted from Paul's words to Timothy: "No one serving as a soldier gets involved in civilian affairs—he wants to please his commanding officer" (2 Tim. 2:4, NIV). The banker was not saying there was anything wrong with a Christian participating in politics; indeed, he had been active in politics. But he believed I should consider this verse in making my decision. That letter proved to be a turning point: if God should so move a busy Christian to write a two-page letter on this subject, I must take his Bible-based counsel seriously.

Communion with God. Carol and I prayed earnestly for those three weeks, expecting that God would want me to run for the legislature. I'm not sure we were always praying according to Mark 14:36—"Not what I will, but what Thou wilt." But down deep we wanted God's will for us.

Contentment. During those three weeks, a terrible burden weighed on my heart. Peace was absent. I had thought that my background and training surely prepared me for this office. Isaiah wrote: "Thou wilt keep him in perfect peace, whose mind is stayed on Thee; because he trusteth in Thee" (Isa. 26:3). For me, it seemed as though contentment would come only by deciding against what I previously thought God was calling me to do.

Circumstances. Contentment seemed to be warring against circumstances. My temporary teaching appointment at the university would soon terminate, and another job would be provided during the election campaign. The timing seemed to be right to plunge into politics. Those were, of course, the superficial circumstances.

Conviction. As I look back, I believe that God used the Holy Spirit, as described in John 16:13: "Howbeit when He, the Spirit of truth, is come, He will guide you into all truth; for He shall not speak of Himself, but whatsoever He shall hear, that shall He speak, and He will show you things to come." The burden that I felt so heavily was the conviction of the Holy Spirit telling me I was not to run for the office.

Careful thought. We know that "God hath not given us a spirit of fear; but of power, and of love, and of a sound mind" (2 Tim. 1:7). I could have carefully analyzed the situation from a human or a divine perspective and arrived at different conclusions. In assessing the pros and cons of making a decision, I have learned to make sure that the divine perspective is well accounted for.

The morning I was to go to the State Capitol in Springfield, I awakened with an enormous burden on my heart. Before getting out of bed, I said to Carol, "God's answer to our prayer is clear; I am not to run for that office." With that, the burden left, and I shouted praises to God as I drove the 90 miles past Illinois cornfields to conduct a state legislative internship program in Springfield.

On some occasions, all seven "Cs" may point in the same direction, but at other times they may lead in opposing directions. What then is the controlling order of these seven principles? The commandments of God must come first. No one can be in the will of God and violate the teaching of God's Word. It is important for us to absorb more of His Word so we can better discern His will.

Often students come to me certain that God's will for them is to date or to marry a non-Christian. That is not even a matter to pray about, for God's Word says NO emphatically to marrying non-Christians. So if you are looking for a marriage partner, why date them? Of course, the response is, "But I can get them converted." Although it's possible, I have never heard of someone converting an unsaved dating or marriage partner. But I have heard of many Christians whose lives have been ruined by dating and marrying an unsaved person.

Ranking next to the commandments of God is communion with God. The link between commandments and communion is made in John 15:7: "If ye abide in Me, and My words abide in you, ye shall ask what ye will, and it shall be done unto you." God's Word conditions our hearts to pray effectively about God's will.

Of course, conviction and contentment are closely linked to commandments and communion. A Christian will not have a conviction to do something that is contrary to the commandments of God. Nor will he have contentment in doing it unless he has hardened his heart to God's Word. In that case, his prayers would not avail anything, because as David said, "If I regard iniquity in my heart, the Lord will not hear me" (Ps. 66:18).

In the next grouping of the seven positive principles, I would place the counsel of Christians, then circumstances, and careful thought. It is very important for any Christian, especially the less mature, to seek counsel from mature Christians. But remember that no one can definitely tell you what God's plan is for you. You have to discover it yourself, with God's help.

A college freshman came into my office about midway through the second semester with a problem about whether to drop a course he was failing. He had come to me for counsel during the first semester about what his major and minor should be. I told him there was no hurry for a freshman to decide, and encouraged him to wait on the Lord to reveal the answers to him. Instead, he rushed into a decision, committing himself to two courses that were not suited to his interests and abilities. The result was the loss of three hours of credit. The young man had sought counsel from his father and me, but he did not follow our advice.

Circumstances can be very important in determining God's will for our lives. Remember Mordecai's challenge to Esther, the Queen. Haman, the right-hand man to King Ahasuerus, wanted to destroy the Jews, and he was skillfully maneuvering the king to have that accomplished. Esther, of course, was a Jewess, and Mordecai challenged her to speak up for her people: "For if thou altogether holdest thy peace at this time, then shall there enlargement and deliverance arise to the Jews from another place; but thou and thy father's house shall be destroyed; and who knowest whether thou art come to the kingdom for such a time as this?" (Es. 4:14)

God is going to get His work done. The question is whether we, like Esther, are going to be in the center of His will helping His cause.

I was asked to speak to a national engineering honor society on "Professional Ethics." I decided to show that the Bible was the foundation of western civilization, and that our civilization is decaying because people no longer adhere to the Bible's ethical standards. Mordecai's words to Esther challenged me: "Who knowest whether thou art come to the kingdom for such a time as this?" Upon finishing that lecture, the audience responded enthusiastically. One professor said there would be one more person in church Sunday morning as a result of the lecture. A divorced professor asked that I start an adult Sunday School class which he could attend. I felt certain that God had put me there for that time.

Although careful thought certainly is scriptural, it can cause us to begin rationalizing away the will of God for our lives. A mind is only "sound" (2 Tim. 1:7) as it is saturated with Scripture. God can trust me to use my mind wisely (Eph. 5:17) if Scripture oils the gears of my mind. That is why the psalmist wrote: "Wherewithal shall a young man cleanse his way? By taking heed thereto according to Thy Word. . . . Thy Word have I hid in mine heart that I might not sin against Thee" (Ps. 119:9, 11). James said that to know the will of God and not do it is to sin against God (James 4:17).

"I pray not that Thou shouldest take them out of the world, but that Thou shouldest keep them from the evil."

John 17:15

4

Living in a Pagan Society

News reports, polls, and statistics continue to remind us of the pagan nature of contemporary society.

• Adultery among national leaders is openly flaunted in the media.

• Wife-swapping among suburban couples is common.

• Divorce rates continue to rise with one in two marriages ending in divorce.

• Policemen now patrol the hallways of many high schools.

• The grasp for wealth continues while poverty haunts sections of rural and urban America.

• Abortion, a disgrace until a few years ago, has become commonplace with an estimated five million babies having been killed in recent years.

• Homosexuality is defended as a natural way of life.

• Child pornography is widespread, causing some state legislatures to pass "anti-child pornography" bills.

• Teachers are leaving their vocation, because undisciplined students threaten and harm them.

• Muggings occur everywhere, even in the neighborhood of the U.S. Capitol and White House.

• Near my home three teenagers lured a married man into a girl's home for illicit sex, where they robbed and killed him.

• A girl who finished the tenth grade with two citations on her police record read about a girl with the same name who had graduated from Vassar. She wrote to Vassar, had her transcript sent to the University of South Carolina Law School, and gained admission. From there she graduated and began to practice law before she was caught. Similar fraud has occurred at Michigan, Harvard, and other universities.

• A student stopped by my office for counsel. His pregnant girlfriend planned to get an abortion and refused to marry him. He opposed the abortion and wanted to marry her. Both professed to be Christians. With her mother's approval and encouragement, she got the abortion.

• One of the better-known Christian evangelists in America left his wife to live with a divorced woman while continuing to try to preach.

Robert Elliot Fitch concluded in *The Odyssey of the Self-Centered Life* that Western civilization has shifted from being God-centered, to nature-centered, to science-centered, and now to self-centered. Rutgers sociologist Peter Berger said, in the spring of 1978, that the United States is a rapidly evolving pagan society.

How do Christians live in a nation that has lost its moral moorings? I have observed four different models: (1) the monk in the monastery, (2) the melting pot, (3) unbalanced enthusiasm, and (4) the moon and sun. Which will get us where we want to go?

Monk in the Monastery

Early one morning in a small Florida town, I was jogging along when I saw two derelicts approaching. Both were sober, but obviously in need of food. After briefly talking with them, I invited them to a restaurant so that I could buy breakfast for them.

The only place open then was a tavern. The men had evidently been denied a handout there and so were planning to walk to the next town several miles away. Sensing how hungry these men were, I took them into the tavern and said I'd buy the two biggest breakfasts available if the proprietor would let me return and pay the tab later. He agreed, so I sat next to the pair while they enjoyed their breakfasts and I told them how Jesus Christ had died to save them from their sins. Although I pressed upon them the urgency of confessing their sins and trusting Christ, they were not ready, but they did promise to go to the skid-row mission in Tampa when they got there.

Later that day I returned to the tavern to pay the owner and to witness to him. I left him a Gospel tract telling how he could be saved.

Some Christians would never have entered that tavern. But it was the only place I could get breakfast for the men. It is certainly not my custom to frequent taverns nor to encourage others to do so. But the important thing was to minister to the physical and spiritual needs of these two men. What kind of witness would I have been if I had not provided them with breakfast? As Jesus said, " 'Lord, when saw we Thee an hungered, or athirst, or a stranger, or naked, or sick, or in prison, and did not minister unto Thee?' Then shall He answer them saying, 'Verily I say unto you, inasmuch as ye did it not to one of the least of these, ye did it not to Me' " (Matt. 25:44-45).

Second Corinthians 6:17 is a hallmark of the monk-in-the-monastery model: "Wherefore come out from among them and be ye separate . . . and touch not the unclean thing." That, of course, is perfectly clear Scripture, but to understand its meaning we should look at John 17:15 where Jesus said, "I pray not that Thou shouldest take them out of the world, but that Thou shouldest keep them from the evil." Separation from the world means spiritual separation, but not always physical separation. Obviously, Christians could never witness if they were physically separate from the world.

It is easy for Christians to follow the monk-in-the-monastery model almost unwittingly in our work, schools, and neighborhoods. We may work with non-Christians, but hardly speak to them, except in passing. In high school and college, we can become so isolated in our Christian organizations that we do not intermingle with the world. And in our neighborhoods, we can live for a lifetime, it seems, without inviting our neighbors to our homes or getting to know them well. The monk-in-the-monastery fails to build bridges to the world so that non-Christians can see the reality of Christian living. I wish that I had built bridges as well in our neighborhood as I attempted to do at work and school.

Another attitude of the monk-in-the-monastery model is: "That's their business if they want to do it." Jonah had that attitude toward the people of Nineveh. He did not care about their eternal destiny, so he tried to avoid taking God's message to them. From Jonah's experience we learn that Christians should be active so that the name of Christ may penetrate all echelons of society.

As a Christian professor on a state university campus, I can do more for Christ among students and professors than if I were a minister, doctor, or a member of any other profession in the community. God is not looking for monks in the monastery, but for witnesses in the world.

Unbalanced Enthusiasm

God usually builds His work slowly. How easily a Christian is tempted to think that the world is rapidly coming to an end and that his life is only a vapor that appears for a while and then vanishes. While both thoughts are scriptural, they may lead us to unscriptural conclusions.

A Clemson University graduate, who had been in my college Sunday School class, left to attend Bible college. In less than nine months, he was planning to establish a state-wide ministry to internationals.

Another student while at Clemson University neglected his studies in the interest of "sharing his faith" on campus. When it came time to graduate and enter Bible College, he was not admitted because he had failed one required course for graduation.

Both students were well-meaning, but forgot key principles about how God builds His work.

Paul emphasized "this one thing I do." Our concentration

should be on the one task God has for us lest we fracture our resources and not make any significant impact. Earlier in my Christian life I made the mistake of thinking about an outreach to all college professors in America. What I overlooked was the necessity of doing my work in my own backyard. As I did, God enlarged my ministry, but it was because of concentration on the limited task of witnessing and discipling one person at a time on my own campus.

In our mania to witness, we may lead many to Christ, but ignore training them. There are several people on my personal prayer list whom I have led to the Lord but who have not grown in the Lord either because I or someone else has not trained them. They aren't doing any good for the kingdom of God, even though they once professed Christ.

Many churches, denominations, and Christian organizations have a large number of "Indians," but not enough trained "chiefs" to lead and teach them. I know of one Christian organization on my campus that avoids attracting large numbers, because they can only teach and train a limited number effectively. As a result, students in other Christian organizations, wanting the in-depth training provided by this group, make an effort to transfer into it.

Ezra's life is instructive on this point. He "prepared his heart to seek the law of the Lord, and to do it, and to teach in Israel statutes and judgments" (Ezra 7:10). Notice that he prepared his heart to do one thing; he did it; and then he was able to teach it to others. Likewise, Nehemiah in rebuilding the walls of Jerusalem would not be dissuaded or distracted from his one task. He said: "And I sent messengers unto them, saying, 'I am doing a great work, so that I cannot come down; why should the work cease, while I leave it, and come down to you?' " (Neh. 6:3)

We can easily be distracted to do many good and worthy things in our mania to please others or to do everything that we see needs to be done. We must remember, however, that although God fully depends on you and me, we are not the only ones on whom He depends.

The Melting Pot

The Apostle Paul wrote about a tragic figure, Demas, who Paul said had "forsaken him, having loved this present world." The Demas syndrome is widely prevalent in Christian churches and organizations. Its slogans typify a cultural Christianity in which culture has more influence on Christianity than the reverse.

To get along, you've got to go along.

Everybody else does it. Why shouldn't I?

Let's not rock the boat.

A little bit won't hurt you.

This model, which seeks to blend in with society, is nearsighted, because God is looking for men and women, boys and girls, who will stand out and be separate from the world. Jesus said: "You are the salt of the earth . . . you are the light of the world" (Matt. 5:13-14). Christians are by definition to be different from the world—different values, different standards, different language, different dress. Paul said that Jesus "gave Himself for us, that He might redeem us from all iniquity and purify unto Himself a peculiar people zealous of good works" (Titus 2:12). Peter wrote: "But ye are a chosen generation, a royal priesthood, an holy nation, a peculiar people; that you should show forth the praises of Him who hath called you out of darkness into His marvelous light" (1 Peter 2:9).

I once knew a professing Christian who, like a chameleon, blended in with whatever the cultural surroundings were. If others were drinking beer, he drank; if they were praying, he prayed; if they were dancing, he danced; if they gossiped, he gossiped; if they read the Bible, he read it. Paul wrote that we should "abstain from all appearance of evil" (1 Thes. 5:22); "All things are lawful for me, but all things are not expedient; all things are lawful for me, but all things edify not" (1 Cor. 10:23). He also wrote that he would not do anything to offend a brother in Christ (Rom. 14:21) and that "you have been called unto liberty, only use not liberty for an occasion to the flesh, but by love serve one another" (Gal. 5:13).

If Martin Luther had followed the melting-pot model, would

there have been a Protestant Reformation? If St. Francis had followed this model, would he have rejected that large inheritance from his father and given the world his example of service? If John Wesley had remained in the Anglican cathedrals, would there have been the revivals of the 19th Century?

The Moon and Sun

Jesus often chose illustrations from nature and the world around Him. The moon and the sun can be constructive models for Christians if we allow for a little literary-scientific license.

Consistency. The moon and the sun appear to move in a set pattern without deviation. That is, there is no compromise. Similarly Christians should not make concessions to the world. John wrote: "Love not the world, neither the things that are in the world. If any man love the world, the love of the Father is not in him. For all that is in the world, the lust of the flesh, and the lust of the eyes, and the pride of life, is not of the Father, but is of the world" (1 John 2:15-16). Peter also put it well when he said: "Abstain from fleshly lusts, which war against the soul" (1 Peter 2:11).

Daniel prayed three times a day and did not deviate from his pattern even though it could have cost him his life. He was thrown into the den of lions because of his prayer life, but God protected him. Note that when he had first been taken into captivity in Babylon long before the test of his prayer life, Daniel "purposed in his heart that he would not defile himself with the portion of the king's meat" (Dan. 1:8).

Comprehension. Consider the sun for a moment. While its main purpose is to give light, it also provides heat and serves as a catalyst in the food-growth process. Because it is light, it does many other things. So too, Christians should give light, but in doing so perform many other functions. Comprehension of our mission involves recognizing that our mission is to light the world just as the sun lights the world in the daytime and the moon at night.

Examination. In a sense, the sun and moon take a daily and nightly test. People look to see if they are shining. In the same way, the world tests Christians. Every day we are tested by the world to see if we are shining. As Christians we certainly must look forward to the judgment when we will be examined by God Himself, but that examination will go well only if we are passing the daily examinations of our life.

Inclination. The challenge confronting the sun is to light the whole world. For the Christian, we likewise must be inclined to accept the same challenge in the spiritual sense. As an untrained person sees it, the sun moves forward without interruption in its movement. Christians are to move forward in the same determined manner. Some Christians see the challenge, but are not inclined to accept it. We must have, therefore, the vision not only to see the challenge, but the determination to accept that challenge.

J. Hudson Taylor, founder of the China Inland Mission, saw the challenge of reaching inland China, and he moved steadily and constantly to accomplish that task. All of his spiritual and physical resources were dedicated toward achieving that one task.

Illumination. What does the sun illuminate? Whatever the atmosphere allows. Similarly, a Christian is to illuminate whatever the atmosphere allows. Clouds may block out the sun's rays, but the light is still there waiting to break through. We too are to be always shining while awaiting the opportunity to shed the light of God on the lives of people in the world.

Such opportunities may not always be expected or immediately understood. While on the faculty at the University of Illinois, I was asked to speak about the effect the proposed Constitution would have on the state of Illinois. At the meeting was a well-known physician whom I had never met. Almost two years passed before he and I finally met in the home of another person. He asked if I had remembered that talk. Then he told me that he had known I was a Christian simply from my demeanor and manner of speaking. That credit belongs to God because He is able to "make all grace abound toward you; that you, always having all sufficiency in all things, may abound to every good work" (2 Cor. 9:8).

Two of my good friends illustrate this point. One of them does not care to hear the good news of Jesus Christ while the other welcomes chances to hear about the Christian faith. I have only rarely witnessed to the former, but hundreds of times to the latter. My light can only illumine that which the atmosphere allows.

Relaxation. From our perspective, the sun and moon shine for half of a 24-hour period and then rest. I had to learn the hard way that I must get a regular, full night of rest and that this is biblical according to Psalm 127:2: "It is vain for you to rise up early, to sit up late, to eat the bread of sorrows: for so He giveth His beloved sleep." It is so easy, especially with fellow Christians, to sit up late talking, particularly when we haven't been together for a long time. But the next day I am not good for much. If our light is to shine every day, we should practice Psalm 127:2 daily. The head of a major Christian organization goes to bed every night at 10:00 unless he is leading someone to the Lord.

A pastor came to one of our discipleship sessions completely exhausted, having done all of those perfectly good things that every pastor should do. But since he had not been getting enough rest, our discipleship session was not of much value to him that day.

Effective witnessing, serving, or any other aspect of the Christian life depends upon a well-rested body. Psalm 127:1 says "Except the Lord build the house, they labor in vain that build it." Regular resting periods are required if we are to serve God properly.

Whenever I lose sleep, such things as irritability and faulty judgment become more common in my life. I am more prone to wander into sin. Isaiah said that "The work of righteousness shall be peace; and the effect of righteousness quietness and assurance for ever" (32:17) and "In quietness and confidence shall be your strength" (30:15). For me, sound and regular sleep is a key to appropriating these promises of God.

Submission. Renegade parents, rebellious children, and revolutionary groups provide more than ample evidence that submission to authority is a touchy subject in today's society. The teaching of Peter is not highly regarded in modern America. "Likewise, you younger, submit yourselves unto the elder. Yea, all of you be subject one to another, and be clothed with humility; for God resisteth the proud, and giveth grace to the humble. Humble yourselves therefore under the mighty hand of God, that He may exalt you in due time" (1 Peter 5:5-6).

The sun and moon must be submissive to their Maker who put them in place to perform a special purpose. They are under His authority. What if they could somehow choose to do something besides what God intended for them? You may say this is not a relevant example since the sun and moon do not have the option of will as we do. But what if they did and chose to do otherwise? Is that not what much of the modern world is doing, choosing to do something God did not intend for them to do? And isn't sin refusing to do something God intends for you to do and refusing to submit to God's authority over you? The results of this sin are seen throughout the world.

"Be sure your sin will find you out" wrote Moses (Num. 32:23). Hosea wrote: "For they have sown the wind, and they shall reap the whirlwind" (Hosea 8:7). Paul wrote: "Be not deceived, God is not mocked; for whatsoever a man soweth, that shall he also reap" (Gal. 6:7).

I grew up under the authority of two interesting parents. My father, at 6' 4" and 250 pounds, would stand toe-to-toe with anyone, and you would have thought that my mother with bright red hair would not back down from anyone. In the context of the modern women's liberation movement, she would have been counseled by many to leave her husband. But she was obedient to God's Word even though my father was not a Christian. In a loving, but firm manner she communicated with my father, and he delegated to her my spiritual rearing, and supported her in all aspects of my Christian training. My father was not the husband he should have been. But my mother was submissive, and in the end, I saw my father's temperament change. Because of my mother's love and submission, he became a Christian before he died. My mother was a liberated woman in the true sense, because she was submissive to the authority of God's Word in her life and to the authority of her husband so long as his authority did not contradict Scripture and cause her to sin. I am very confident that my mother's humble submission to authority is directly responsible for my walk with the Lord today.

"Then said Jesus to those Jews which believed on Him, 'If you continue in My word, then are ye My disciples indeed.'"

John 8:31

5

Governed by the Word

After listening to me and making only sparse comments for about 30 minutes, the man looked me straight in the eye and said "The verse of Scripture you need is Ezra 7:10." That verse was like a sharp arrow directly aimed at my heart.

I had gone to Washington, D. C. on a business trip during a crucial time in my life when I was wrestling with the idea of entering full-time Christian service as a minister. A close Christian friend, after hearing of my concern, said he wanted me to talk with a wise Christian about the matter. It was this second Christian friend who quoted Ezra 7:10 at the close of our conversation. "For Ezra had prepared his heart to seek the law of the Lord, and to do it, and to teach in Israel statutes and judgments."

With his counsel and God's Word sharply penetrating my heart, I returned home committed to being like Ezra. Ezra was not a priest, but a government official—yet greatly used of God as a leader and teacher. During the next few years God sent over 2,000 college students for me to teach in a Sunday School class, opened the doors of approximately 100 churches for preaching and teaching opportunities, and granted a counseling ministry with both college students and adults.

Obviously this man counseled me with the right verse of Scripture, because he had become absorbed in God's Word. God used him and his knowledge of Scripture to convict and penetrate my life. His heart was like a quiver full of sharp arrows of Scripture. This wise man had come to know what the Bible is and how it should govern one's life.

What Is the Bible?

Many people do not seek to be governed by the Bible because they really do not know what it is. They believe it to be the Word of God, but they really do not know its purposes, claims, and functions. When people really know what the Bible is, they want it to govern their whole lives. Jeremiah said, "Thy words were found, and I did eat them; and Thy Word was unto me the joy and rejoicing of mine heart; for I am called by Thy name, O Lord God of hosts" (Jer. 15:16). As Jeremiah found out what God's Word was, he wanted it to take total control of him. We are shaped by what captures our senses. Jeremiah desired to have God's Word to stimulate and control his senses.

Purposes, Claims, Functions. When teaching a seminar on how to let the Bible govern us, I am amazed at how people's faces light up as they see for the first time a comprehensive picture of what the Bible says about itself. To give a capsule presentation, I show the information on figure 1 on an overhead projector. Usually the seminar then comes alive. Most of these people in the seminars have been Christians for years, but many have never viewed a comprehensive picture of what the Bible is. Many Christians are treading water to keep from drowning. They don't know that the lifeguard's rope nearby can be used to pull them ashore if they will only grab onto it.

Jesus and the Bible. Besides knowing what the Bible says about itself, I have found it equally important to know the relationship between Jesus and the Bible. It would appear that over 90 percent of all Christians know little about the crucial relationship between the two. John 1:1 and Revelation 19:13 teach that the Bible and Jesus are identical in essence though they differ in form. That is, the Bible is God's Word in written form while Jesus is God's Word in bodily form.

John 1:1, 14—"In the beginning was the Word, and the Word

was with God, and the Word was God. . . . And the Word was made flesh, and dwelt among us, (and we beheld His glory, the glory as of the only begotten of the Father,) full of grace and truth."

Revelation 19:13—"And He was clothed with a vesture dipped in blood; and His name is called The Word of God."

People in these seminars are fascinated by how the Bible develops this relationship. Figure 2 reveals the identical nature of Jesus and the Bible with respect to their characteristics and ministries and also with respect to our responsibilities toward them.

Figure 1

A Capsule Picture of the Bible

What It Is		*Functions*	
1. Eternal	Isa. 40:8	1. Feed	Job 23:12
2. Inspired	2 Tim. 3:16	2. Sanctify	Eph. 5:26
3. Judging	John 12:48	3. Illumine	Ps. 119:105
4. Sacred	Prov. 30:6	4. Purify	Ps. 119:9
5. Pure	Ps. 12:6	5. Instruct	Deut. 4:10

Not to Be Maligned
Rev. 22:18-19

Purposes		*Claims*	
1. Present Jesus	John 20:31	1. Flame	Jer. 5:14
2. Give Hope	Rom. 15:4	2. Hammer	Jer. 23:29
3. Give Examples	1 Cor. 10:11	3. Life	Ezek. 37
4. Give Knowledge	1 John 5:13	4. Power	Rom. 1:16
		5. Weapon	Eph. 6:17
		6. Discerner	Heb. 4:12

Figure 2

Jesus and the Bible: Their Identical Natures

Character	Bible	Jesus
TRUTH	John 17:17	John 14:6
LIFE	John 6:33	John 11:25
COUNSEL	Ps. 119:24	Isa. 9:6
ETERNAL	Matt. 24:35	Heb. 1:10, 11
LIGHT	Ps. 119:105	John 8:12
SHIELD	Ps. 91:4	Prov. 30:5
PRECIOUS	2 Peter 1:4	1 Peter 2:7
PURE	Ps. 12:6	1 John 3:3

Ministry	Bible	Jesus
REGENERATE	1 Peter 1:23	John 1:12, 13
FREE	John 8:32	John 8:36
SANCTIFY	John 15:3	1 John 1:9
DISCERN	Heb. 4:12	Heb. 4:13
INDWELL	Col. 3:16	John 15:3-4
CREATE	Heb. 11:3	John 1:3
JUDGE	John 12:48	2 Cor. 5:10
PEACE	Isa. 48:18	Eph. 2:14
FAITH	Rom. 10:17	Heb. 12:2
STRENGTH	Zech. 8:9	Phil. 4:13

Responsibility*	Bible	Jesus
FEED	Jer. 15:16	Ps. 34:8
LOVE	Ps. 119:97	John 14:21
OBEY	1 Sam. 15:22-23	John 15:10
PREACH	2 Tim. 4:2	Acts 3:20
MEDITATE	Ps. 1:2	Ps. 63:6
GLORIFY	Ps. 138:2	2 Thes. 1:10
INDWELL	Col. 3:16	John 15:4-5

*Our personal responsibility to the Bible and to Jesus

Reading Evaluation. Once a person has this comprehensive picture of the Bible and also of its relationship to Jesus, it is much easier to be excited about having the Bible govern the whole of one's life. When Dwight L. Moody made his commitment to the Word, he determined insofar as possible to read only the Bible and books that helped illumine passages of the Bible. I used to regularly read four to six newspapers a day. Although I still appreciate the importance of newspapers, I spend far less time with them and much more time with God's Word, because newspapers are ephemeral while the Bible is eternal. Many people major on reading books about the Book, but spend little time with the Book itself. They are majoring on minors about the Bible rather than majoring on the Bible itself. Two questions are very important to me. Do I spend more time reading secular literature than I do sacred literature? Do I spend more time reading books and articles about the Bible than I do studying the Bible itself?

Goals for Bible Study.

Having the Bible govern my life has become a much more meaningful and real goal since I learned to appreciate what the Bible is. We are to be disciples; Jesus said, "If you continue in My Word, then are you My disciples indeed" (John 8:31). Being a disciple means continuing in the Word of God.

We should desire to be obedient to the Word of God by studying it as Paul wrote to Timothy: "Study to show thyself approved unto God, a workman that needeth not to be ashamed, rightly dividing the Word of truth." (2 Tim. 2:15) The word *study* means "be diligent" or "do your best." The only approval anyone should seek is God's approval and that comes when we are diligent in the study of His Word, understanding or "rightly dividing it." Both explicit and implicit throughout Scripture is that study of the Word and doing the Word are linked. (See Ezra 7:10.) James 1:22 reads: "But be you doers of the Word, and not hearers only, deceiving your own selves." We deceive ourselves when we only hear, but do not do the Word of God.

Another purpose of our study and application of God's Word is that we may grow, just as Peter wrote: "As newborn babes, desire the sincere milk of the Word, that you may grow thereby" (1 Peter 2:2). This growth should continue as it did in Ezra's life so that we become teachers of the Word. There is a serious danger in failing to become a teacher of the Word. It is as though atrophy has set in and we lose use of part of our body. When a part of the body has not been used for a period of time, the use is lost until it is gradually developed again. A 100-yard-dash man cannot quit running for a year and expect to return immediately to his former speed. Likewise, spiritual strength cannot be stored without use. Hebrews 5:11-14 says:

Of whom we have many things to say, and hard to be uttered, seeing ye are dull of hearing. For when for the time ye ought to be teachers, ye have need that one teach you again which be the first principles of the oracles of God; and are become such as have need of milk, and not of strong meat. For every one that useth milk is unskillful in the word of righteousness: for he is a babe. But strong meat belongeth to them that are of full age, even those who by reason of use have their senses exercised to discern both good and evil.

We should also seek to be governed by the Word because it is the only redeeming truth, as Jesus said: "And you shall know the truth, and the truth shall make you free" (John 8:32). Later He prayed: "Sanctify them through Thy truth; Thy Word is truth" (John 17:17). God's Word is the measure of all knowledge. Anything at variance with Scripture is not true. Isaiah 8:20 reads: "To the law and to the testimony: if they speak not according to this word, it is because there is no light in them."

Why should we invest in anything that does not last forever when we can invest in something that does? Peter wrote: "For all flesh is as grass, and all the glory of man as the flower of grass. The grass withereth, and the flower thereof falleth away: But the Word of the Lord endureth for ever" (1 Peter 1:24-25).

Why should we seek to be governed by the Book? Dwight L. Moody once said: "Either sin will keep you from this Book, or this Book will keep you from sin." That has certainly been true in my life. Whenever I wander from the Book, sin has entered my life in thought, word, or deed. But my desire to read the Book increases as I seek God's holiness. Not only does the Bible attract our attention when we come to realize what it is, but also when we desire its cleansing power.

Letting the Bible Govern You

The average person retains 10 percent of what he reads, 20 percent of what he hears, 30 percent of what he sees, 50 percent of what he hears and sees at the same time, 70 percent of what he is able to describe in his own words, and 90 percent of what he discusses and performs of what he had read, heard, or seen. (TIM-151, Department of Industrial Education, University of Texas)

One very significant fact should be noted about this data. Retention increases as more of our senses become involved in the learning process. If we really want the Bible to govern us, we must let all of our senses be exposed to the Bible and come under its authority.

1. Law of biblical gravity. Sometimes the expression is used that a person is well grounded in the Word. Just as there is a physical force of gravitation, so too is there a spiritual force of gravitation. Isaac Newton said that the force of gravity is determined in part by the weight of the object and its proximity to the earth. The biblical weight of the Christian and his proximity to being grounded in the Word are determined by six elements.

• *Reading the Word.* "Blessed is he that readeth, and they that hear the words of this prophecy, and keep those things which are written therein; for the time is at hand" (Rev. 1:3).

• *Hearing the Word.* "So then faith cometh by hearing and hearing by the Word of God" (Rom. 10:17).

• *Studying the Word.* "Study to show thyself approved unto God, a workman that needeth not to be ashamed, rightly dividing the Word of truth" (2 Tim. 2:15).

• *Memorizing the Word.* "Thy Word have I hid in mine heart, that I might not sin against Thee" (Ps. 119:11).

• *Meditating on the Word.* "But his delight is in the law of the Lord; and in His law doth he meditate day and night. And he shall be like a tree planted by the rivers of water, that bringeth forth his fruit in his season; his leaf also shall not wither; and whatsoever he doeth shall prosper" (Ps. 1:2-3).

• *Doing the Word.* "But be you doers of the Word, and not hearers only, deceiving your own selves" (James 1:22).

The more these elements of biblical gravitation are in our lives, the greater our spiritual weight and, therefore, the nearer we will be to God's perfect standard for us, which is total grounding in the Word of God.

2. *Problem areas.* "I just don't seem to understand the Bible." "So much of it simply doesn't make sense." "It seems to be so dull and boring." These reactions are common among many people and may usually be traced to one or more of four problem areas. Each of these areas also affects the others. For example, if I am spiritually prepared to study the Bible, but am studying it in the wrong place, with the wrong methods and at the wrong pace, I will not accomplish much.

• *Spiritual preparation.* Ezra prepared his heart to seek the law of the Lord, to do it, and then to teach it (Ezra 7:10). His example teaches us that our spiritual preparation involves a total commitment to going all the way with the Word of God. A halfhearted commitment will not unlock the storehouse of wisdom and knowledge in His Book. God wants to reveal the depth of His truths to those who are committed to doing and teaching His Word, not just knowing what it says.

To be spiritually prepared we must have Scripture absorb us all the time. "This Book of the Law shall not depart out of thy mouth; but thou shalt meditate therein day and night" (Josh. 1:8). I try to have my last thoughts before going to bed at night and my first thoughts before getting out of bed in the morning on God's Word. I read God's Word and review verses I have memorized before going to bed and then I try to think of a verse I am memorizing when awaking in the morning. Often I meditate on that verse at odd moments during the entire day.

• *Logistics.* "Pen in motion reflects mind in gear." This is a proverb that I made up a few years ago to impress upon my students that exam grades in my classes usually correlate pretty closely with the quantity and quality of a student's notes. For me, the early morning time when I am really fresh is my best time to study God's Word with paper and pen in hand. For several years I have been in the process of studying the Bible through so that I will have my own personal notes on every chapter in the Bible. The place that I use is my library at home. It causes that room to have special meaning to me, because that is where God has revealed so much of Himself to me. Logistically I think it is important for a person to have a certain time, a certain place, and certain equipment—pen and paper—to enhance one's understanding of Scripture. My children have come to realize without being told that early morning in my study is a very special time and place for me.

• *Methods.* My morning Bible study is only one method that I use to get into God's Word. In any given day, I may use several methods, including hearing, reading, memorizing, and meditating. There is no reason to become bored with the Bible since there are so many methods to approach it. Besides these basic methods, I have found it helpful to use other methods.

Biographical method wherein I may study the life of a personality in the Bible

Doctrinal method to determine what the Scripture has to say, for example, about the doctrine of salvation

Word method to determine where and in what contexts a particular word is used in the Bible

Topical method to learn what the Bible has to say about a subject like death or hell

Verse-by-verse method to analyze a particular passage of Scripture in depth

Over the years I have built a library that helps me to learn more about Scripture, particularly to understand difficult passages. I do not buy many books, generally only those that will be useful as reference tools to help with problems of scriptural interpretation.

For example, the issue of mode of baptism once arose in a church to which I belonged, so I turned to *Vine's Expository Dictionary of New Testament Words* to determine where and how the word was used and what its meaning is in the Greek.

There are four simple rules that I have used in studying Scripture that have helped me overcome problems of interpretation. First, I ask what the *general theme* is of the passage under consideration. Second, I note the *general principles* being taught in the passage. Third, I seek to note what cross-references reinforce my interpretation of the passage; that is, I *compare Scripture with Scripture*. Fourth, I *check reliable sources* if in doubt about my interpretation. By following these four steps I have never had any difficulty in properly interpreting Scripture.

There are also some impromptu ways of appropriating Scripture to our lives, such as being constantly alert, while in conversation, for Scriptures that relate to topics being discussed. I do not always use the Scriptures that come to mind, but at least my mind is alert to what God's Word says about the subject. Then if I don't have a Scripture memorized on the subject, I make note of that so that I will not be caught without a Scripture on that subject again.

• *Pace.* Continuous and slow with variation in method! If I become a little tired of Scripture memory, I just increase the amount of time I devote to Bible study, but regardless, I am always applying one or more methods. Thus, I never become tired or bored with the Bible. I have also learned that one should be like the turtle rather than the rabbit in getting to know the Bible—just be slow, but sure. A too hasty approach yields poor results. I have learned that God builds slowly and surely so that a solid foundation is laid. I don't try to memorize too much Scripture a week, because I really would not be able to absorb a large amount properly. For the new Christian I recommend one to two verses per week which if reviewed and meditated upon during an entire week will become much more a part of a person than if one memorized a long passage.

As a child between the ages of 6 and 12, my mother led me in the memorization of literally hundreds, perhaps thousands, of verses of Scripture. She wanted my life to be built on a solid foundation, since she recognized the truth of Psalm 37:31—"The law of his God is in his heart; none of his steps shall slide."

"And whatsoever we ask, we receive of Him, because we keep His commandments, and do those things that are pleasing in His sight.

1 John 3:22

6

Barristers at the Bar of Heaven

The acute pain caused me to roll on my bed in agony. Not knowing the cause, but believing it was very serious, I asked my wife to call the doctor and ask him to meet me in the hospital emergency room.

Thinking that I would be confined to the hospital, I asked my wife to bring my Bible, Scripture memory cards, and Bible study guide and then I began to pray during the 30-minute trip, stretched out in the back of our station wagon with our apprehensive children looking on.

Somehow I couldn't pray much for myself, because I believed that God would take care of me physically. I felt burdened to pray that God would give me at least one man in the hospital whom I could lead to Jesus Christ.

The emergency room, packed to overflowing on Friday night with accident, knifing, and shooting victims, had no space available so the nurse directed me to the waiting room. As I stumbled out to wait, another nurse saw my ashen face and said: "Stop, I want to take your pulse." By that time, my pulse had dropped to the low 40s, and immediately space was made available in the emergency room.

For almost two days, the doctors waited for my pulse to return to normal, and then surgery was ordered for Monday morning. At about 6:00 on Sunday morning, two orderlies came into the room. One noticed that I was studying the Bible, so he asked if I were a preacher. I told him I wasn't and after a brief conversation I continued my study.

On Monday morning, I was awake early for Bible study and prayer when that same orderly returned to prepare me for surgery. The preparation was quite painful, but it was during the height of the pain that the Lord enabled me to lead him to trust Jesus Christ as his Lord and Saviour.

The following two nights when he was on the graveyard shift from 11 P.M. to 7 A.M., he stopped by my room to receive instruction about how to grow spiritually.

I believe there were reasons that God answered my prayer to lead someone to Himself.

Preparing to Plead at the Bar

I had been a Christian for 26 years when I became ill. Sadly, during much of that period I really did not know about the importance of proper preparation to pray. So often prayers are not answered because we have not properly prepared. Indeed, I believe our preparation to pray is as important, if not more so, than our actual prayers.

There are four key elements in preparing to pray: our manner of coming, our attitude in coming, our personal life before coming, and the condition of our heart and mind.

1. Manner of coming. Scripture teaches us to come to prayer wholeheartedly, boldly, quietly, and specifically.

"And ye shall seek Me, and find Me, when ye shall search for Me with all your heart" (Jer. 29:13).

"Let us therefore come boldly unto the throne of grace, that we may obtain mercy, and find grace to help in time of need" (Heb. 4:16).

"Be still, and know that I am God" (Ps. 46:10).

"Hitherto have you asked nothing in My name: ask, and you shall receive, that your joy may be full" (John 16:24).

During the beginning of the "black power" movement, I stood in a New York restaurant catering exclusively to blacks, in one of the city's most densely populated black areas. I had gone there to get some sandwiches for several of us who were attending a meeting nearby with a nationally known black politician. As I stood there, two very strong and tall black men came up to me and said in threatening voices, "Black power!" What should I do? Run? They would easily catch me. Punch them? Utter foolishness! Talk back? Ridiculous. As wholeheartedly as I could and with all boldness, but quietly, I specifically asked God in the name of Jesus to protect me. God immediately led me to offer to shake their hands, to introduce myself and to ask them how they were. For reasons known only to God, the two men were pacified, and we began to have a friendly conversation.

Wholeheartedly means that our attention is entirely focused on the purpose of our prayer. *Boldly* means that we are forthrightly, not timidly, coming into His presence. *Quietly* means that we are waiting for God to answer rather than seeking human answers to our need. And *specifically* means that our prayer is made in the name of Jesus.

Boldly and *quietly* are not contradictory, in that *boldly* reflects our forthrightness and *quietly* our trust in God alone. A person praying loudly may or may not be praying with a quiet spirit of trust. Both our boldness and our quietness reflect our confidence in God. "In quietness and in confidence shall be your strength" (Isa. 30:15).

As I prayed on that 30-minute trip to the hospital emergency room, these prayer prerequisites had been met. God knew that I meant business. How easy it would have been to pray about the intense pain and the danger of serious surgery that lay ahead of me.

2. Attitude in coming. My mother's life offers many examples of excellence in prayer preparation, but perhaps none better than the time mentioned earlier when her life was at stake. Her doctor had said that X rays showed a growth the size of a baseball in her side and that surgery was needed immediately. My mother called to tell me about the doctor's recommendation and then quickly added that she was not going to follow it. Her 92-year-old mother needed her attention at her home some 200 miles away, and she was going there to care for her. In a very relaxed manner, she said: "Charles, don't worry, God will take care of me. When I return from caring for my mother, I will go to the hospital for surgery." My strongest protests were of no avail.

A few weeks later, my mother reported to the hospital for surgery, and X rays were once again made. The result was that the large growth had disappeared, and she went home without surgery.

My mother knew that God wanted her to care for her mother. She trusted God to care for her own physical needs since she was putting God first, others second, and herself third. Her attitude consisted of seeking God and His desires (Ps. 27:8), of being humble before Him (2 Chron. 7:14), of accepting His will in a relaxed manner (Phil. 4:6-7), of being submissive to His dictation to her (1 Peter 5:6-7), and of placing all her hope in God (Heb. 10:19-22). The last passage of Scripture warrants our full consideration here, because it expresses so well the attitude we should have.

Having therefore, brethren, boldness to enter into the holiest by the blood of Jesus, by a new and living way, which He hath consecrated for us, through the veil, that is to say, His flesh; And having an high priest over the house of God; let us draw near with a true heart in full assurance of faith, having our hearts sprinkled from an evil conscience, and our bodies washed with pure water. Let us hold fast the profession of our faith without wavering; (for He is faithful that promised).

3. Personal life before praying. It is very doubtful that our prayers will be heard and answered if we cannot answer each of the following questions in the affirmative.

• Have I been obedient to God's Word? (1 John 3:22)
• Have I been hearing God's Word preached? (Prov. 28:9)
• Have I been resisting sin? (Ps. 66:18)
• Have I been helping the poor? (Prov. 21:13)
• Have I been forgiving others? (Mark 11:25)
• Have I as a husband, been caring for and treating my wife properly? (1 Peter 3:7)

• Have I been doing God's will in all areas of my life? (1 John 5:14)

For example, speaking as a husband, I can testify most certainly that if I have not treated my wife kindly my prayers are of no avail. It is easy for a husband to hold hidden grudges if he thinks his wife has not done something properly. Such an attitude will adversely affect his prayer life.

One of the reasons my mother has had such a successful prayer life is that she has always, despite her own poverty, helped the poor. All of her life she worked as a maid or a janitress, but somehow from her meager resources she managed to help those less fortunate.

I have heard people say they do not need to go to church to hear God's Word preached, but I have never known one of these persons to be a successful prayer warrior.

4. *Condition of heart and mind.* I was teaching a four-night series in a Presbyterian church on the need for Christians to strive for the mastery (1 Cor. 9:25). A young husband became very upset when I said that troubles in the home so often originate with the husband and that we as husbands have a special responsibility under God to care for our wives as Christ cared for the church (Eph. 5:25). With a very critical attitude, he spoke out sharply against me and the teaching he had just heard. I thanked him for his comment and continued teaching. Later the pastor's wife expressed her appreciation for how the situation was handled, but speculated that the young husband, who had serious spiritual problems, would not be back. I simply said that I would be praying for the young man. This incident troubled me because I did not want to be tearing apart their church.

That night my family and I knelt for our nightly session of prayer, and we brought this young man before the throne of grace. The next day I prayed many times that the young husband would be there that night and with a teachable spirit. That night the prayer was answered.

I believe the reasons God answered that prayer are laid out in Scripture. *First,* God's Word is to condition our hearts and minds before we pray. "If you abide in Me and My words abide in you, you shall ask what you will, and it shall be done unto you" (John 15:7). My heart and mind had been conditioned by much study of the Scriptures in preparation to teach God's Word. *Second,* James wrote, "The effectual fervent prayer of a righteous man availeth much" (James 5:16). The prayer was certainly fervent, and I had for some time been striving by the grace of God to live a righteous and holy life. *Third,* I knew God heard my prayer (1 John 5:15), and *fourth,* I believed He would answer it (Matt. 21:22). *Fifth,* I thirsted for God to answer the prayer. The psalmist put the idea of thirst very well: "O God, Thou art my God; early will I seek Thee; my soul thirsteth for Thee, my flesh longeth for Thee in a dry and thirsty land, where no water is" (Ps. 63:1). *Sixth,* I was praying for something big, something unexpected. (Jer. 33:3). I was praying for a change in this man's attitude and desire within a 24-hour period. Not even the pastor's wife expected that.

Importunity at the Bar

Early one Sunday morning as I was shaving, I heard a knock on the bathroom door. It was my son Joshua, then age four, without a stitch of clothing on him. I said, "Joshua, what do you want?"

He replied, "Daddy, I just want to give you a big hug and tell you I love you."

I melted. His shameless desire to express his affection for his father brought tears to my eyes. If he had wanted anything that day, his prospects for getting it were pretty good. He had touched my heartstrings.

When Joshua saw his brother, two years older, get his first bicycle, he asked for one. Then as he would see another child about the same age with a bicycle, he would ask again. He used every strategy and all the tactics a child could muster to persuade me that he needed a bicycle right then. His persistence was unfailing.

Often I have been deeply moved by Joshua's pleas for his older brother, trying to stop me from spanking him, arguing that his brother needed whatever it was he wanted, crying that we should not leave until Charlie comes. In short, he is willing to take on himself his brother's needs and burdens.

Perhaps these are among the reasons why Jesus said: "Except ye become as a little child, ye shall not enter the kingdom of heaven." A child will often shamelessly and persistently represent both his and others' interests.

Importunity, only used once in all of Scripture (Luke 11:8), comes from the Greek word *anaida,* and means "shameless persistence."

How thrilled I was one Sunday morning to see a young man step out of his place, grasp the hands of his wife and children, and walk to the front of the church to see the pastor. His wife as well as many other people had prayed shamelessly and persistently for several years for this husband and father that he would get right with God. I recall crying as I prayed for him some mornings on my knees. When he turned to speak to the congregation, I could not contain a "Praise God."

The idea of importunity is well expressed by Isaiah, who said, "You that make mention of the Lord, keep not silence, and give Him no rest, till He establish, and till He make Jerusalem a praise in the earth" (Isa. 62:6-7). Isaiah mourned that "there is none that calleth upon Thy name, that stirreth up himself to take hold of Thee" (Isa. 64:7).

Approaching the Bar

There are three important considerations in how we approach the bar of heaven: the time, the place, and the methods. Paul said to "pray without ceasing" (1 Thes. 5:17). It was said of Charles Haddon Spurgeon that he could shift so smoothly from conversation to prayer that it was hardly noticed. The spirit of prayer had evidently such control over him that he was almost always in the spirit of prayer even in normal conversation. Prayer is certainly not limited to one time and one place and one method, but certain times, places, and methods are probably better than others.

1. Time of Prayer. Read the Book of Joshua and count the number of times Joshua rose early in the morning to meet with God. David thought so much of prayer in the morning that he advocated it twice in the same verse (Ps. 5:3). Jesus practiced early morning prayer (Mark 1:35). Giants of the faith have down through the years used the early morning hours for prayer. Luther prayed two hours every morning except on busy days when it was three hours. Wesley rose at 4 A.M. to pray for two hours, and Bishop Asbury likewise. I try to talk with God in the morning before anyone else in the family wakes up. In that way I have prayed thoroughly for God's guidance for them during that day, as well as for other matters.

2. Trysting place. Where can God count on you to meet with Him regularly in prayer? I like to be in my library on my knees. Sometimes I walk to avoid drowsiness and wandering thoughts, but usually I prefer being on my knees. The library takes on a special meaning for me, because that is where I do business with God. That is where I praise and thank Him and plead my case before Him. My only regret is that I did not start having a special place to pray sooner in life and that I do not spend more time there.

3. Methods. Either explicitly or implicitly, several methods of prayer are taught in Scripture. While all are important, I believe Christians use the methods of praise and thanksgiving far less and prayers of supplication (petition) far more than they should. With respect to prayers of confession, we take this method too lightly by asking God to forgive us of our many sins rather than to name our sins one by one. We should be very specific with God so that we can realize how much God is really forgiving us. Of course, we should realize that all sin, regardless of what it is, is sin against God. David said: "Against Thee, Thee only, have I sinned, and done this evil in Thy sight" (Ps. 51:4).

Praising God at the start of my prayer time takes my mind off myself and my personal needs and focuses on God and how great He is. This begins the process of recognizing that God is certainly more than able to answer my petitions. The psalmist said: "Great is the Lord, and greatly to be praised; and His greatness is unsearchable'' (Ps. 145:3). It is helpful to me to think of a verse of praise and then to praise God for each of His attributes mentioned in the verse. Such as, ''The Lord is my rock, and my fortress, and my deliverer; my God, my strength, in whom I will trust; my buckler, and the horn of my salvation, and my high tower'' (Ps. 18:2).

Second, after praising specifically for several of His attributes, I begin *confessing sin* in my life. How can I afford to have any unconfessed sin in the presence of such a great and glorious God? ''If we confess our sins, He is faithful and just to forgive us our sins, and to cleanse us from all unrighteousness'' (1 John 1:9). My confession and God's forgiveness accentuate the greatness of God and my own unworthiness, causing me to see even more clearly my dependence on Him.

Third, I *thank God* for specific answers to prayer and for His abundant mercy and grace. This helps me to focus on God's faithfulness. Paul wrote, ''Giving thanks always for all things unto God and the Father in the name of our Lord Jesus Christ'' (Eph. 5:20).

Fourth, I *petition* God with my needs and requests. By this time, my appreciation for who God is and what He has done has increased my faith. I am able to pray in a believing attitude because I know that He will hear and answer my prayers. It is here that I pray for both large and small requests, beginning with the needs in my home and then extending to the need of my neighborhood and beyond until I am praying for foreign missionaries.

In making our petitions, we should state the best possible case for why we want the petitions answered by God. That is, we should argue with God, but not in the sense of being unwilling to accept His answer. As Job said, ''I would order my cause before Him, and fill my mouth with arguments. I would know the words which He would answer me, and understand what He would say unto me'' (Job 23:4-5).

I have used several forms of prayer, including secret (Matt.

6:6), group (Acts 2:42-47), conversational, without words, and fasting (Mark 9:29).

Prayer in my trysting place is *secret prayer* unless one of my children comes in, but then what a joy to close my morning prayers with one or more of them at my side on their knees. Those are glorious mornings.

I have found that *group prayer* helps to encourage and strengthen everyone in the group and to remind them of one another's needs, just as it did in the early church. I always appreciate hearing the prayers of older Christians who have prayed so many more times than I, because they pray with such assurance and meaning. A form of group prayer, *chain prayer,* was perhaps made famous by a group of Moravians who determined that they would pray for 100 years in such a manner, so that at no time during the day or night would the chain of prayer be broken. On several occasions I have had a part in organizing prayer chains so that over a 24-hour period or longer someone would always be in the sanctuary praying. Within groups *conversational prayer,* with each one praying only a short sentence or two at a time, but praying more than once, helps to create a feeling of group cohesion and also to remind one another of needs and to collectively lift those up to God.

Particularly when with a group of people not engaged in prayer, I may *pray without words* as my mind and heart are engaged in prayer. Frequently this type of prayer arises because of an urgent need. I have seen God dramatically answer prayer at times like these, protecting me or others from harm or changing the spirit of a cantankerous person.

Jesus said: "This kind can come forth by nothing, but by *prayer and fasting*" (Mark 9:29). His reference here is to those with great spiritual power. Jesus Himself fasted, and we are to be His disciples. Can we do any less? I am not sure anyone can fully explain the mystery of fasting, but I can say it works if we follow Jesus' instruction about fasting in secret (Matt. 6:16-18). In fasting for the first time, I recommend that a person (1) fast over a 24-hour period when one's mind is generally not occupied with work or other concerns, (2) spend a substantial portion of that time in prayer and Bible study, (3) eat a light meal before beginning the fast, (4) drink generous amounts of water during the fast, and (5) eat a light meal such as a tossed salad and fruit juice when ending the fast.

4. Prayer List. To make my prayer time more effective and efficient, I maintain a prayer list to help guide me. Although not slavishly followed, the prayer list helps me to be better organized and to pray regularly about matters that might otherwise be forgotten. Of course, it is thrilling to thank God for an answer and then to strike through that item on the prayer list.

I keep my prayer list on several 3″ x 5″ note cards. I can carry these cards with me to use at other times, such as in a taxicab or in a doctor's office. Listed on the cards are several types of requests: personal, neighborhood, church, missionaries, unsaved friends, and special concerns or requests. Periodically I have to type up new prayer cards, because the old ones become worn, and then the old ones serve as reminders of God's faithfulness to me.

Regardless of one's maturity in prayer, I think the example of Jabez' boldness is inspiring. "And Jabez called on the God of Israel, saying, 'Oh that Thou wouldest bless me indeed, and enlarge my coast, and that Thine hand might be with me, and that Thou wouldest keep me from evil, that it may not grieve me!' And God granted him that which he requested" (1 Chron. 4:10).

"So thou, O son of man, I have set thee a watchman unto the house of Israel; therefore thou shalt hear the word at My mouth, and warn them from Me. When I say unto the wicked, 'O wicked man, thou shalt surely die;' if thou dost not speak to warn the wicked from his way, that wicked man shall die in his iniquity; but his blood will I require at thine hand. Nevertheless, if thou warn the wicked of his way to turn from it; if he do not turn from his way, he shall die in his iniquity; but thou hast delivered thy soul."

Ezekiel 33:7-9

7

Watchman on the Wall

A few minutes before 8 A.M. classes were to begin during my sophomore year in high school, I stood in the hallway talking with a group of friends when a student came running down the hall, shouting to me, "Charlie, did you hear what happened last night?"

The news spread with lightning speed. Pat had died. I had played on the football, basketball, and baseball teams with him. Most importantly, though, I had witnessed to him, telling him that he needed to trust Jesus Christ as his Lord and Saviour.

Pat's sudden death from leukemia saddened me, especially since I had no reason to believe he had trusted Christ. My only consolation was that I had at least witnessed to him.

But what if I had not witnessed to Pat? I was thinking of the Lord's words to Ezekiel: "His blood will I require at thine hand" (Ezek. 33:8).

What greater responsibility could one have than to be appointed by God as a watchman on the wall of the world, not only to warn people of their impending doom but also to show them there is a perfect way of escape?

A witness is one who testifies to what he has seen, heard, and knows. A witness in court, of course, swears to tell the truth about what he has seen, heard, and knows. When we trust Jesus Christ as Saviour, we come under orders to testify to the truth of Jesus Christ. Jesus said: "You shall be witnesses unto Me" (Acts

1:8). And John clearly specified the nature of the witness or testimony in 1 John 1:1-3:

> That which was from the beginning, which we have heard, which we have seen with our eyes, which we have looked upon, and our hands have handled, of the Word of life; (for the life was manifested, and we have seen it, and bear witness, and show unto you that eternal life, which was with the Father, and was manifested unto us;) that which we have seen and heard declare we unto you, that you also may have fellowship with us; and truly our fellowship is with the Father, and with His Son Jesus Christ.

The importance of our witness cannot be more strongly emphasized than to know the Greek derivation of the word, *martus* from which we get the word *martyr*. A martyr is one who gives his life for his testimony. Witnessing is serious business. We are to be willing to give our lives to the cause of witnessing for Christ.

By definition, a witness must be verbal. You and I may perform many good deeds, but how are others to know that we are performing them in the name of Jesus Christ? We may also have excellent attitudes in difficult circumstances, but again how are others to know that our attitudes result from the saving grace of Jesus Christ? As John wrote, "That which we have seen and heard declare we unto you" (1 John 1:3). Declaration requires verbalization.

How to Witness

The Bible teaches that we are to witness boldly, unceasingly, unashamedly, knowledgeably, constantly, and universally. Why did the early believers multiply so rapidly? Very simply, they met each of these criteria.

Boldness. The early believers were sound in doctrine, consistent in fellowship, and fervent in prayer (Acts 2:42). As a result of their common doctrine, consistency in fellowship, and fervency in prayer, they had boldness.

My wife and I were once members of a church not meeting these criteria for boldness. Not surprisingly, I had little boldness in my own life, because I was adversely affected by the church. Then we left to affiliate with a church that met these criteria, and our boldness and desire to witness intensified immediately.

The word *bold* in its various forms is prominent in the Book of Acts and should not be overlooked as a principal reason for the rapid multiplication of their number. Many Christians lack boldness today because many churches do not meet the conditions of boldness.

Believers in the Book of Acts had an inward fire that would not be quenched. Just as Jeremiah said: "His word was in mine heart as a burning fire" (Jer. 20:9). This inward fire would not let them be content with anything less than a bold and clear witness for Jesus Christ.

After delivering a message I have called, "My Last Lecture" (chapter 11 of this book) at the College of Liberal Arts Convocation at Clemson University, a faculty member followed me to my office, repeating over and over: "Do you realize what you did?" He said that it was one of the boldest lectures he had ever heard.

From my perspective, I could have never delivered the lecture in my own power, but by God's grace I was granted the boldness to do so. My lecture tested my faith in Christ against scholarly critics and intellectual antagonists, showing that even in their own words Jesus reigns supreme. Some walked out, others were offended, some would not speak to me for several weeks, but the majority were appreciative. Long hours in Bible study, much prayer and consistent fellowship provided the necessary boldness to deliver the lecture to faculty and students.

Unashamed. Paul wrote to Timothy: "Be not thou therefore ashamed of the testimony of our Lord" (2 Tim. 1:8). Fear of what others will say or think about us frequently discourages us from witnessing. The early believers knew that Jesus Christ had died for their sins, had risen again from the dead, and that they had seen Him ascend into heaven. Their hearts and minds were focused on exactly what ours should be. As we meditate more on what Jesus Christ did for us, can we make any sacrifice too great for Him? Witnessing, of course, should not be considered a sacrifice, but a privilege. He has ordained us as ambassadors to represent Him in this world, and far from being just a privilege, it is also the greatest honor we could have (2 Cor. 5:20).

Knowledge. Paul had been a Christian for many years when he told the Corinthians: "I delivered unto you first of all that which I also received, how that Christ died for our sins according to the Scriptures and that He was buried, and that He rose again the third day according to the Scriptures" (1 Cor. 15:3-4). The newest Christian can witness to those facts as well as to the fact that he has trusted Jesus Christ and is now a new person in Him. Witnessing is not a matter of waiting until we have great knowledge.

On the other hand, it is important for us to acquire knowledge, especially biblical knowledge, that will enhance our witnessing. The following outline presents a systematic analysis of salvation from Scripture. I have used it many times to witness to people from diverse walks of life. I sit down with a blank sheet of paper and a Bible and develop this outline as the person to whom I am witnessing reads designated verses and answers my questions, in the development of the outline.

Systematic Analysis of Salvation

1. What is grace?
   A. Free gift—Romans 6:23
   B. Cannot be earned—Titus 3:5

2. Who is man?
   A. A sinner—Ecclesiastes 7:20
   B. Cannot save himself—Romans 3:20

3. Who is God?
   A. Holy—Leviticus 19:2
   B. Merciful—Romans 5:8
   C. Just—Exodus 34:7

4. Who is Jesus?
   A. God and man—John 1:1, 14, 18
   B. God's provision for man's sins—Isaiah 53:6

5. What is faith?
   A. Not simply believing something is true—James 2:19
   B. Trust—Proverbs 3:5-6
      1. Believe—John 1:12
      2. Surrender—Luke 9:23
      3. Obey—John 14:21
   C. Prerequisites to exercising faith
      1. Confession of sin—1 John 1:9
      2. Repentance (turning from) of sin—Mark 1:15; Luke 13:3

6. Why is the blood of Christ important?
   A. No forgiveness without shedding of blood—Ephesians 1:7; Colossians 1:14; Hebrews 9:22
   B. Basis of justification—Romans 5:9

7. How is salvation assured? 1 John 5:11–13; John 5:24; Romans 10:9–10; John 3:16

8. What is the purpose of salvation? Ephesians 2:10; Titus 2:14; 1 Peter 2:9

9. When should one be saved? Isaiah 55:6; 2 Corinthians 6:2; Hebrews 3:15; Proverbs 27:1

10. What is the price of rejecting salvation? Hebrews 2:3; Luke 13:3; Romans 6:23; John 3:36

Far too many people and witnessing plans overlook two key points that are fundamental to salvation. The first one is *repentance*. Jesus' first recorded words in Mark are, "The time is fulfilled, and the kingdom of God is at hand; repent ye, and believe the Gospel'' (Mark 1:15). Repent means to "turn from.'' In our witnessing we must tell people that they are to turn from their sins. Confession is not enough. When we fail to tell people that repentance is a necessary prerequisite of salvation, we create the illusion of "easy believism"—that being a Christian does not require any major changes in their lives.

Secondly, we overlook the blood of Jesus Christ. Hebrews 9:22 reads in part: "Without shedding of blood is no remission.'' People must be told that Christ's blood washes away their sins. Romans 5:9 reads: "Much more then, being now justified by His blood, we shall be saved from wrath through Him.''

In addition to having this biblical knowledge of salvation, we need to witness to what God has done in our lives. The psalmist said: "I will declare what He hath done for my soul" (Ps. 66:16). And Isaiah said: "I will mention the lovingkindness of the Lord" (Isa. 63:7).

Finally, we should always be ready to bear witness with the knowledge we have. Peter said: "But sanctify the Lord God in your hearts; and be ready always to give an answer to every man that asketh you a reason of the hope that is in you with meekness and fear" (1 Peter 3:15).

Constant. Once a person is appointed as an ambassador of a government, he does not cease to be one until his ambassadorial mission is completed. As Christians, our mission on earth is not completed until we die or Jesus comes to get us at His second coming. We are to witness unceasingly. "You that make mention of the Lord, keep not silence" (Isa. 62:6). Acts 4:20 records the words of Peter and John: "For we cannot but speak the things which we have seen and heard.'' Our witness is to be unceasing, because we should have an irrepressible urge to witness. It was said that John Wesley would quicken his stride to catch up with a total stranger and witness to him while walking.

Universal. Since we are to be constant and unceasing witnesses, we are to witness everywhere just as Jesus told those gathered with Him at the time of His ascension. "You shall be witnesses unto Me both in Jerusalem, and in all Judea, and in

Samaria, and unto the uttermost part of the earth" (Acts 1:8). We do not have the right to pick and choose the place of our witness, but rather we are to be witnesses wherever God places us.

I have had exciting witnessing opportunities on airplanes and trains, in taxis and buses, on street corners, and in numerous other places. I have developed the habit of handing out tracts to strangers as an expression of my concern that they know the truth about Jesus Christ. Only one person, a derelict outside the New York Hilton, has ever seemed unappreciative of receiving a tract from me.

While hurrying to get a plane at New York's LaGuardia Airport, I overheard one ticket agent, a young man, teasing another ticket agent, a young woman, about her "night life." In a very humorous way, he asked her questions as she protested that he really did not know anything about her "night life." With only moments to spare, I handed the young woman a tract entitled, "Am I Going to Heaven?" and suggested that she ask the young man a more important question. Her face lighted up and she said: "This is just what I need." As I hurried off to the plane, the two were engrossed in reading the tract.

Witnessing Attitudes and Analogies

Jesus' comparison of witnessing to fishing provides an excellent understanding of the attitudes a witness should possess. He of course, said: "Follow Me, and I will make you fishers of men" (Matt. 4:19). Anyone even remotely exposed to a fisherman knows that almost all fishermen possess common attitudes. These are:

1. a great desire and love for fishing
2. willingness to spend long hours doing it
3. continual study to improve their skills and success
4. use of the best methods possible
5. a deep love to talk about their fishing experiences
6. endurance of adverse circumstances to fish
7. sensitivity to where the fish are biting
8. relaxation while they fish

9. willingness to get up early to go fishing
10. willingness to go anytime, day or night.

Jesus chose the fishing analogy probably because of attitudes stated above. We know also that fishing is a universal activity understood around the world; moreover, fishing differs from hunting in a very distinct way. In the former, the fish decide to swim into the net or to bite the hook, but in the latter, the animal has no choice. As fishers of men, we simply put out the net or the hook, but we cannot force the Gospel message on anyone. That is the job of the Holy Spirit of God.

Jesus used several other analogies that reveal what kinds of witnesses we should be. Significantly, each of these analogies shown in figure 3 is a penetrating agent of some type that accomplishes a specific result.

Figure 3

Jesus' Analogies to Witnessing

Example	Scripture	Result
Salt	Matthew 5:13	Seasons/Preserves
Light	Matthew 5:14	Banishes darkness
Keys	Matthew 16:19	Unlocks the door
Bread	John 6:33, 35	Strengthens body
Water	John 4:10-11	Makes earth habitable
Leaven	Luke 13:21	Improves/Builds up
Fire	Luke 12:49	Cleanses

Results of Witnessing

For the faithful witness there is great reward. I shall never forget the excitement of leading that first person to the Lord Jesus Christ. And each time is just as exciting, which is as it should be according to Scripture, since Jesus said that "joy shall be in heaven over one sinner that repenteth" (Luke 15:7).

But for the witness specifically, the psalmist wrote: "He that goeth forth and weepth, bearing precious seed, shall doubtless come again with rejoicing, bringing his sheaves with him" (Ps. 126:6). Daniel said: "And they that be wise shall shine as the brightness of the firmament; and they that turn many to righteousness as the stars for ever and ever" (Dan. 12:3).

"For whom the Lord loveth He chasteneth, and scourgeth every son whom He receiveth . . . Now no chastening for the present seemeth to be joyous, but grievous; nevertheless afterward it yieldeth the peaceable fruit of righteousness unto them which are exercised thereby."

Hebrews 12:6, 11

8

The Surgeon's Scalpel

I had just snuggled into bed when the phone rang. A long distance caller told me that a man for whom I had been praying at least two years had trusted Jesus Christ as Saviour and that he wanted me to disciple him when he returned from vacation.

At that time I had never discipled anyone in my life. What was I to do? Recalling a discipleship training program given to me sometime before, I quickly dusted it off to help rescue me.

That experience gave me a new and challenging opportunity to be used of God to train men individually in how to live the Christian life. Since then I have been involved in training many men, including ministers, college professors, teachers, businessmen, and students.

Prior to this first experience, I had taught and preached before large audiences and worked with small groups. But I had never trained a new Christian to pray, to study and to memorize Scripture, to witness, and to disciple others.

A Disciple's Goals: Separation and Sanctification

A *disciple,* from the Greek word *mathetes,* literally means "a learner." In the Christian context, a disciple is to learn to be like Christ as Paul said: "Let this mind be in you, which was also in Christ Jesus" (Phil. 2:5).

What was it that Jesus specifically wanted His disciples to learn? Perhaps no better answer can be found than in Jesus' prayer for His disciples in John 17: "I pray not that Thou should take them out of the world, but that Thou would keep them from the evil" (John 17:15). This means separation from sin.

How is a disciple to keep himself separated from sin in the world? Two key words in Jesus' prayer in John 17 provide us with the answer: *world,* used 19 times, and *word,* used 5 times. As John recorded, a disciple is to be *recruited* out of the world, *trained* in the Word, and *sent* into the world.

> I have manifested Thy name unto the men which Thou gavest Me out of the world: Thine they were, and Thou gavest them Me; and they have kept Thy Word. For I have given unto them the words which Thou gavest Me; and they have received them, and have known surely that I came out from Thee, and they have believed that thou didst send Me. As Thou hast sent Me into the world, even so have I also sent them into the world.
>
> (John 17:1, 8, 18)

Jesus said, "Sanctify them through Thy truth; Thy Word is truth" (John 17:17). The process of separation from sin involves sanctification or purification through the Word of God. Peter gave the formula for living separated lives, the basis of which is the Word of God and the goal of which is a fruitful life.

> According as His divine power hath given unto us all things that pertain unto life and godliness, through the knowledge of Him that hath called us to glory and virtue: Whereby are given unto us exceeding great and precious promises: that by these ye might be partakers of the divine nature, having escaped the corruption that is in the world through lust. And beside this, giving all diligence, add to your faith virtue; and to virtue knowledge; and to knowledge temperance; and to temperance patience; and to patience godliness; and to godliness brotherly kindness; and to brotherly kindness charity. For if these things be in you and abound, they make you that ye shall neither be barren nor unfruitful in the knowledge of our Lord Jesus Christ.
>
> (2 Peter 1:3-8)

Sanctification and the Word are clearly linked in Ephesians 5:26-27: "That He might sanctify and cleanse it [the Church] with the washing of water by the Word, that He might present it to Himself a glorious Church, not having spot, or winkle, or any such thing; but that it should be holy and without blemish." To be sanctified requires that a person not only accept the Bible as God's Word, but that he also be willing to come totally under its authority. Many people accept the Bible as the Word of God but they don't come totally under its authority. They apply only those scriptural truths that are convenient for them to obey.

For example, a church with which I am familiar claims to believe that biblical standards are authoritative in governing the church. But this church has conveniently overlooked the biblical necessity of disciplining members engaged in conduct such as adultery, which is clearly prohibited by Scripture, and for which the Bible says discipline is to be imposed.

In addition to instruction about separation from the world, the Bible also states very specifically the kind of activities or people from which we are to separate ourselves in keeping with the admonition to "abstain from all appearance of evil" (1 Thes. 5:22) and "as strangers and pilgrims" to "abstain from fleshly lusts, which war against the soul" (1 Peter 2:11).

First, Paul exhorted the Romans: "Now I beseech you, brethren, mark them which cause divisions and offenses contrary to the doctrine which ye have learned; and *avoid them*" (Rom. 16:17).

Second, to the Corinthians he wrote: "But now I have written unto you *not to keep company*, if any man that is called a brother be a fornicator, or covetous, or an idolater, or a railer, or a drunkard, or an extortioner; with such an one, no, not to eat" (1 Cor. 5:11).

Third, Paul not only mentioned specific types of people from whom the Corinthian Christians were to separate themselves but also explained the reasons why:

Be ye not unequally yoked together with unbelievers: for what fellowship hath righteousness with unrighteousness? And what communion hath light with darkness? And what concord hath Christ with Belial? Or what part hath he that believeth with an infidel? And what agreement hath the temple of God with idols? For you are the temple of the living God; as God hath said, "I will dwell in them, and walk in them; and I will be their God, and they shall be My people. Wherefore come out from among them, and *be you separate,*" saith the Lord, "and touch not the unclean thing; and I will receive you, and will be a Father unto you, and you shall be My sons and daughters," saith the Lord Almighty (2 Cor. 6:14-18).

Fourth, he told the Thessalonians to *"withdraw yourselves* from every brother that walketh disorderly, and not after the tradition which he received of us" (2 Thes. 3:6).

Fifth, Paul further exhorted: "If any man obey not our word by this epistle, note that man, and *have no company* with him, that he may be ashamed" (2 Thes. 3:14).

Sixth, Paul warned Timothy:

If any man teach otherwise, and consent not to wholesome words, even the words of our Lord Jesus Christ, and to the doctrine which is according to godliness; He is proud, knowing nothing, but doting about questions and strifes of words, whereof cometh envy, strife, railings, evil surmisings, perverse disputings of men of corrupt minds, and destitute of the truth, supposing that gain is godliness; from such *withdraw thyself* (1 Tim. 6:3-5).

Seventh, Paul enjoined Christians to separate from several types of persons: "lovers of their own selves, covetous, boasters, proud, blasphemers, disobedient to parents, unthankful, unholy, without natural affection, trucebreakers, false accusers, incontinent, fierce, despisers of those that are good, traitors, heady, highminded, lovers of pleasures more than lovers of God; having a form of godliness, but denying the power thereof." Paul said, *"From such turn away"* (2 Tim. 3:2-5).

Eighth, Paul taught: "A man that is an heretic after the first and second admonition *reject"* (Titus 3:10).

Ninth, John admonished Christians to separate from one who

"abideth not in the doctrine of Christ. . . . If there come any unto you, and bring not this doctrine, *receive him not* into your house, neither bid him God speed; for he that biddeth him God speed is partaker of his evil deeds" (2 John 9-11).

Sanctification of Christlike qualities internally and separation from evil externally should be the disciple's goals.

Scripture is replete with examples of the fate of those who failed to be obedient to Scripture. Consider Moses in the wilderness when the Israelites were suffering from thirst. Moses was to "speak unto the rock" so that it would give forth water to the people. Instead, Moses "lifted up his hand, and with his rod he smote the rock twice." Water did come forth, but Moses had disobeyed God's Word by striking the rock. For Moses' sin, God said he could not enter the Promised Land (Num. 20:8, 11-12). Moses had done great good for the people. They now had water, but he had done the good in the wrong way.

In 1 Samuel 6:13-20, the Bethshemites not only rejoiced when the Ark of the Covenant was returned from the Philistines, but they also offered burnt offerings and sacrifices. All of this was good except that they violated the command of God not to look into the Ark of the Covenant. As a result, thousands were slain. The people of Bethshemesh then asked: "Who is able to stand before this Holy Lord God?" The answer, of course, is in Psalm 24:3-4 which reads: "Who shall ascend into the hill of the Lord? or who shall stand in His holy place? He that hath clean hands, and a pure heart; who hath not lifted up his soul unto vanity, nor sworn deceitfully."

After Saul had disobeyed God by not completely destroying the Amalekites and by keeping certain of their possessions ostensibly for sacrifices to God, Samuel rebuked Saul and told him he had lost his kingship. Samuel's words were: "Hath the Lord as great delight in burnt offerings and sacrifices, as in obeying the voice of the Lord? Behold, to obey is better than sacrifice, and to hearken than the fat of rams" (1 Sam. 15:22).

Lest one should think this is purely Old Testament teaching, Jesus' words should be considered: "He that hath My commandments and keepeth them, he it is that loveth Me" (John 14:21). Our love for God is demonstrated by our obedience to all of His commandments.

An Instrument of the Surgeon

Who is the discipler? He is merely one instrument of the Surgeon, God.

There is emphasis these days on a one-to-one relationship that may breed pride on the part of the discipler and dependence on the part of the disciples. Of course, neither 2 Timothy 2:2 nor 1 Corinthians 3:6-9 allows for these unhealthy relationships.

For example, Paul said to Timothy: "And the things that thou hast heard of me among many witnesses, the same commit thou to faithful men, who shall be able to teach others also" (2 Tim. 2:2). Paul told Timothy that he had learned about the Christian life from many people, Paul being just one, and that he (Timothy) should pass along those things to others. A surgeon, of course, uses many instruments, and Paul was merely one of God's instruments in training Timothy.

Then to the Corinthians, Paul wrote:

I have planted, Apollos watered; but God gave the increase. So then neither is he that planteth anything, neither he that watereth; but God that giveth the increase. Now he that planteth and he that watereth are one: and every man shall receive his own reward according to his own labor. For we are laborers together with God: ye are God's husbandry, ye are God's building (1 Cor. 3:6-9).

His message reinforced his admonition to Timothy, namely that discipleship is more than just one man training one man. The discipler should seek to have a disciple exposed to many Christians, especially in the context of a Bible-believing church. In such an environment he will grow faster because he has been exposed to more than one source of food and water. The men I have trained have done much better and have been much less dependent on me when they have been involved in a church that met the criteria of the Early Church in Acts, such as sound doctrine, close fellowship, fervent prayer, personal discipleship, bold witnessing, and strong unity.

One man whom I led to the Lord would not respond to personal discipleship training. But when he affiliated with a doctrinally sound church he developed Christian maturity without the benefit of man-to-man training. As I reflect on his situation, I believe that he was not suited to personal discipleship. In fact, I believe that the importance of personal discipleship for all Christians may be overestimated. The rapid growth of the believers in Acts certainly suggests that one-to-one discipleship was not intended for everyone. In my own life, I was never discipled personally by another man, but like Timothy I have been trained by many people.

Three other men whom I discipled had different growth rates because of different church experiences. The first did not follow my suggestion that he affiliate with a Bible-believing church, and the result was a dampening of his spiritual enthusiasm. He lost his keen interest in Scripture memorization, Bible study, and witnessing. The second man remained in a lukewarm church contrary to my counsel and he, too, lost his spiritual zeal. The third man left the same lukewarm church to affiliate with a sound, Bible-preaching church and his zeal increased. As a result of these experiences, I now disciple only those men who will affiliate with churches adhering to the fundamentals of Scripture. There is too much risk and potential waste of time in training men who will not affiliate with a church that adheres to the fundamentals of the faith.

Many have wondered if a Christian should try to infiltrate a biblically unsound church to try to change it or if he should separate from it. Twice in my life I thought I could remain in churches and help rescue them and their denominations from the encroachments of false doctrine. Once I taught a Sunday School class where people started to bring their Bibles for the first time. I was excited because I thought we had made real progress. Attendance increased and their enthusiasm grew. But now, several years later, I see that those people and their pastor were not affected by my efforts. On another occasion I became a denominational officer and spoke widely in the denomination, but without effect. It was then that I awoke to the truth of Scripture: infiltration is not taught; separation is.

God's injunction is to separate from sin, including churches that do not hold to the inerrancy and authority of Scripture. No matter how much good we may think we can accomplish in a church that does not adhere to God's Word, we are still to separate. Romans 3:8 teaches that it is wrong to disobey God in order to have a chance to do right. Scripture could not be more clear. In the Bible, obedience always leads to separation from sin regardless of the form of sin.

Several questions may be helpful in evaluating the spiritual fiber and doctrinal orthodoxy of a church. (1) Do the pastor and church leaders believe in the total inerrancy and full authority of Scripture? (2) Do the church leaders, including the pastor, meet the biblical criteria for holding their positions? (3) Does the missions budget constitute a substantial portion of the church budget? (4) Does the missions budget support only missionaries, or does it support also colleges and seminaries? If so, are all professors at those schools and their teaching consistent with the church's position on the inerrancy and authority of Scripture? (5) Are church members exhorted and trained to witness? (6) Does the church minister to the physical as well as the spiritual needs of people in the community? (7) Are people being saved through the church's witness?

Some might question why so much space has been devoted to the church in a chapter on discipleship. "Church," mentioned 119 times in the New Testament, is one of the most dominant doctrines in the Bible. Of those 119 times, 90 are specific references to the local assembly or gathering of believers. If Jesus Christ died for the church and if God saw fit to place so much emphasis on the church in Scripture, then do we have any right to neglect that which God has chosen to exalt?

A disciple should be taught to fully and enthusiastically participate in the life of a local church. That, of course, does not mean only "tipping one's hat" to the church by perfunctory attendance on Sunday morning. The New Testament reveals, for example, that a church congregation is to meet regularly and often for such purposes as worship, prayer, teaching, and preaching and that all believers are to participate.

The disciples, except for Thomas, were meeting on Sunday night after the crucifixion when Jesus appeared and said, "Peace be unto you" (John 20:19). How sad Thomas must have felt to have missed that first appearance of Jesus! When told by the other disciples that Jesus had met with them on Sunday night, he said: "Except I shall see in His hands the print of the nails, and put my finger into the print of the nails, and thrust my hand into His side, I will not believe" (John 20:25).

If only Thomas had not been absent from the Sunday night meeting, he would not have had to suffer Jesus' rebuke eight days later when Jesus said, "Thomas, because thou hast seen Me, thou hast believed; blessed are they that have not seen, and yet have believed" (John 20:29). Many times I have told other Christians how God is working in our Sunday night and midweek services, only to hear them respond in unbelief as Thomas did. They have missed the blessing of the very presence of God and, like Thomas, their lives show it.

As a result of observing several college and university ministries on three campuses over many years, I have seen many Christian students falter upon graduation because the campus ministry either did not encourage full and enthusiastic participation in a local church or neglected to teach them to identify with a biblically-sound church. A local church is the best and most likely place to receive continued nurture as a Christian over a lifetime, but if a student or anyone else is not taught this very important factor in discipleship, he has a spiritual Achilles heel—he is vulnerable to defeat.

How to Choose a Disciple

Discipleship means learning, and the disciple is necessarily learning from someone else. Therefore, either directly or indirectly one person is going to be teaching another person what to do. Paul put it very succinctly: "Those things, which ye have both learned, and received, and seen in me, do: and the God of peace shall be with you" (Phil. 4:9).

Is a person teachable, that is, willing and able to receive and apply instruction from another person? It is patently fruitless to disciple someone who is unwilling to be taught what to do and then to apply that instruction.

If a person is willing to obey God's Word and then to be taught in the Word, one can be certain he will also meet the other criteria for a disciple as taught in 2 Timothy 2:2-4—faithfulness, endurance of hardship, and availability. One test I give to determine if a person meets these criteria is simply to ask him to meet with me at 6:30 A.M. once a week for several weeks.

Jesus said that "except a corn of wheat fall into the ground and die, it abideth alone; but if it die, it bringeth forth much fruit" (John 12:24). The seven metamorphic changes in a grain of wheat parallel the growth of a Christian to full maturity as a fruit-bearing disciple of Jesus Christ, and they are also good signs that confirm disciple potential. They are:

1. softening of the grain of wheat upon being placed in the soil
2. enlarging of the grain of wheat as it begins to grow
3. changing of its chemistry from starch to sugar
4. breaking of the hard shell so that root formation can begin
5. growing of roots downward to develop a root structure to support a plant above ground
6. growing of a sturdy green shoot above ground
7. bearing of fruit.

I have been told of an experiment wherein one grain became 32,500 grains within three years, but it is significant to note that most of this development takes place underground. The first five metamorphic changes occur there. I find it interesting that the Apostle Paul spent some three years, essentially unaccounted for in Scripture, away from the center of public attention. It was during this time, relatively alone, that he developed the root structure necessary to support his phenomenal ministry. Perhaps that is why Paul admonished Timothy to "lay hands suddenly on no man" (1 Tim. 5:22).

Choosing a disciple requires constant attention to the spiritual metamorphosis in a disciple's life. Some, for example, can be like two men, a bartender and a convict, both of whom I led to the Lord.

The bartender came forward during a public invitation. I dealt with him and pointed out the necessity of repentance. When we got on our knees to pray, he broke down as he called out to God for mercy. The next week he quit his job and began to be trained in the faith. But after a few months his enthusiasm waned, and he returned to his bartending job despite strong counsel and rebuke from me.

I went to the county jail to witness to the convict who was soon to be sentenced to prison on a serious drug charge. About a week later, he professed faith in Christ, but he would never take any steps to grow in the faith. In fact, his profession could have been influenced by his desire to obtain a lenient sentence.

Choosing a disciple is a dynamic and not a static process. The man I trained who has been the most successful fruitbearer appeared least likely to pass through all the metamorphic changes. He had come from a church where regular attendance was for social reasons, and the minister never preached the necessity of repentance and conversion. Already well established in his career, he had no readily apparent reason to change his lifestyle. Yet he kept moving toward the disciple's goal: "Christ in you, the hope of glory; whom we preach, warning every man, and teaching every man in all wisdom; that we may present every man perfect in Christ Jesus" (Col. 1:27-28). There were occasions when I rebuked him sharply (Titus 1:13) and admonished him sternly, but he responded positively each time. On the other hand, a man I would have chosen as being a more natural disciple let his pride get in the way—he rebelled at the idea of someone else teaching him what to do.

Paul had similar experiences. Demas, for example, forsook him, "having loved this present world" (2 Tim. 4:10).

Apparently Demas had a good start but was not able to finish the rugged course of discipleship.

The Windmill

What should the disciple be taught? Of course, this whole book focuses on various teachings a disciple needs to receive. But the parallels between discipleship and a windmill offer an excellent way of depicting what a disciple should learn. (This illustration was originally brought to my attention by a football player whom I was discipling.)

First, a windmill is designed to catch the wind with the greatest efficiency. The Greek word for wind and spirit are the same. Thus, a disciple's life is to be built and to function in order to enhance the power and efficiency of the work of the Holy Spirit.

To operate efficiently, a windmill must have a sturdy foundation to support large, wind-catching blades. Those blades that harness the Holy Spirit's power in a disciple's life are the Bible, witnessing, prayer, and fellowship.

Since the wind is a source of power, the blades must be covered properly to allow the wind to propel them without damaging them. If a disciple's blades are not covered properly, then he will be deficient in one or more of the crucial sources of power. Lack of prayer, for example, would subject a disciple to a damaged life and lack of spiritual power.

The miller must constantly watch the direction of the wind in order to position the blades properly. To assist him, an apparatus is fixed to the ground that allows him to turn the windmill to face the wind. In the same way, the disciple must always be grounded in the Word in order to know the direction he should face in life.

Also, the miller must be ready to work when the wind blows, day or night, so that the unseen source of power may be harnessed. Likewise, a true disciple is always ready to share the Good News (1 Peter 3:15).

Finally, the windmill's work always begins in the position of a cross. In this way, the blades may be prepared by the miller from the ground. For many years, millers attached spiritual significance to covering the blades while they are in the cross position. Of course, just the right amount of fabric must be placed on the blades, depending on the wind's velocity. Likewise, a disciple is to begin each day at the Cross in order to properly prepare for the day ahead. Jesus said, "If any man will come after Me, let him deny himself, take up his cross daily, and fellow Me" (Luke 9:23).

"Casting all your care upon Him; for He careth for you."

1 Peter 5:7

9

Worry Conquered

The hour was late. My son Charlie, then five years old, tossed and turned in his bed as I wondered why he was not going to sleep. After checking him several times, I finally asked him why.

Charlie answered: "Daddy, a big boy said he was going to kill me."

Our church then had a "Round-Up" ministry on Saturday mornings primarily for underprivileged children, and we wanted Charlie to participate so he could make new friends and understand how they lived. Coming from rowdy backgrounds, they often would speak of killing someone and not mean it, but in our home the word was rarely used. So Charlie, who understood neither their background nor language, was deeply worried.

I said, "Charlie, what does Philippians 4:6-7 say?"

Charlie then quoted it: "Be careful for nothing; but in everything by prayer and supplication with thanksgiving let your requests be made known unto God. And the peace of God, which passeth all understanding, shall keep your hearts and minds through Christ Jesus."

Then I asked Charlie what he should do, and he said: "Pray, and not worry." We did, and Charlie immediately went to sleep. The next Saturday the big bully became Charlie's friend.

On another occasion, at age six, Charlie worried about passing his swimming test. He fretted and said he did not want to take the test for fear of failing it. Once again I asked him to quote

Philippians 4:6-7, and then to pray. He immediately stopped worrying, and his fretful countenance became radiant with happiness. But young boys are not the only ones who worry.

What is Worry?

In the Greek, worry means "to divide, part, rip, or tear apart." Its principal biblical synonyms are anxiety and care. To worry is to become unduly concerned about something we can do nothing about.

Human emotions are God-given, and are therefore good if properly used. Hatred is good if we use it to hate evil. Anger is good if it is righteous indignation. Concern is good so long as it does not become obsessive worry. In effect, worry is fretting about a problem God has not given us the resources to solve.

The dictionary defines worry as "mental distress or agitation resulting from concern, usually for something impending or anticipated."

Worry, of course, is sin, because when we worry, we violate clear commandments of Scripture. For example:

"Casting all your care upon Him: for He careth for you" (1 Peter 5:7).

"Be careful for nothing" (don't be anxious or worry about anything, Phil. 4:6).

"Take therefore no thought for the morrow" (do not worry about tomorrow, Matt. 6:34).

"Thou wilt keep him in perfect peace, whose mind is stayed on Thee," (Isa. 26:3).

In both examples, Charlie was worried about what might happen without really knowing what would happen. He, of course, did not know that the big bully regularly used the word *kill* in his home neighborhood without really meaning it. Jesus said in the Sermon on the Mount, "Therefore, do not worry about tomorrow, for tomorrow will worry about itself. Each day has enough trouble of its own!" (Matt. 6:34, NIV).

In the second example, Charlie was worried about a test several days away. He did not know how difficult the test would be nor did he recognize that passing that test at age six or age seven really made little, if any difference. Moreover, he had several days to practice for the test.

In both cases, Charlie was worried about something he could not change and something about which he did not know all the facts. Worry was tearing him apart.

Of course, we also worry about things which have already happened, second-guessing ourselves as to whether we acted properly. We have no control over the past. Although we can plan for the future, we certainly cannot control it. Certainly, we should learn from the past, but not brood about it.

Worry debilitates us and sometimes incapacitates us. In Charlie's situations, he was becoming nervous and could not sleep, resulting in a loss of energy, both physically and emotionally.

What Causes Worry?

In the summer of 1978, a May graduate of Clemson University called and asked to see me. His girlfriend had just jilted him, and he was deeply distressed. His ego, as he put it, had been crushed. The young man's situation illustrates one of the principal causes of worry, fear.

Fear. He feared his girlfriend's reaction, he feared his personal limitations, he feared that he could not change the situation. Circumstances, other people, and personal limitations may cause us to worry, and then we become ensnared by them, causing us to think only about these things. That, of course, is one of the lessons of Proverbs 29:25: "The fear of man bringeth a snare." God's Word teaches us to fear God only so that our minds will be freed of worry about our personal situation to think and meditate about God and His resources for us.

Proverbs 1:7 reads: "The fear of the Lord is the beginning of knowledge; but fools despise wisdom and instruction." Proverbs 9:10 reads: "The fear of the Lord is the beginning of wisdom; and the knowledge of the holy is understanding." When we fear God only, we begin to receive the wisdom and knowledge necessary to cope with our personal problems that might otherwise plague us with worry.

Envy. I once knew a person who, when denied the position he wanted, expressed his envy of the person who did get it by retreating into a shell, neither speaking to the person who got the position nor to the persons responsible for the selection. Significantly, neither the person who got the job nor the selection committee had anything personal against him. They respected his professional and personal capabilities. However, for several years the man isolated himself, punishing himself as he worried about his lot in life, but thinking he was hurting others by his withdrawal from them. After several years, he began to make friends again, and his colleagues were most happy to help him in every way. "Wrath is cruel, and anger is outrageous, but who is able to stand before envy?" (Prov. 27:4) Envy totally consumes a person, causing one not to understand reality.

Comparison with Others. Any analysis of envy as a cause of worry leads to its root problem, comparing oneself with others. The result is unhealthy competitiveness.

I have known of preachers who worried about another preacher's church being larger, and college presidents who worried about the growth of competing institutions. Two of history's most famous preachers were notoriously envious of the other's church to the point that when one sent "a token of peace" to the other, he rejected it. I once heard a college president in a chapel service devote much of his message to castigating another Christian institution which, incidentally, was experiencing a greater growth rate and more recognition. He indicated that a school growing that fast had suspicious standards. His worry about his own institution led him to deny the power of God being responsible for the growth of the other school.

No one is immune from the temptation to worry by comparing oneself with another. Businesses and salesmen often overextend themselves and sometimes go bankrupt or incur serious loss because they worry about getting ahead or staying ahead of another company or person. Girls, envious of another's looks, worry about ways to bring the other girl down to their level. *Laziness*. Every semester, students tell me how worried they are about final exams. After a few questions, I soon discover that most of them have not studied regularly and rigorously during the semester. They have spent too much time dating or in the student union building or some other place. They have procrastinated.

Anyone who puts off doing what can and should be done presently faces a pile of things to worry about ultimately. The housewife who neglects cleaning the kitchen ends up with a major job on her hands. The salesman who neglects making calls faces a low commission.

God wants us to be victorious over our problems, not besieged by worry. Paul pointed us to the solution to worry: "Nay in all these things we are more than conquerors through Him that loved us" (Rom. 8:37).

How to Conquer Worry

The causes of worry are obvious to most people, but the cure is often a mystery. A simple formula can help eliminate most, if not all, causes of worry. First, one should know God's promises. Second, one should know the difference between planning and worrying. Third, one should have a procedure for dealing with worry.

When the newly graduated senior came into my office worried about his girlfriend jilting him, I first led him to understand that worry is sin which must be confessed and repented of. Then I quoted several verses to show how ridiculous it is for the Christian to worry:

"God is my strength and power; and He maketh my way perfect" (2 Sam. 22:33).

"The Lord is good, a stronghold in the day of trouble; and He knoweth them that trust in Him" (Nahum 1:7).

"And call upon Me in the day of trouble; I will deliver thee, and thou shalt glorify Me" (Ps. 50:15).

As I quoted these and other verses, the young man grabbed his pencil and started to write down the references, asking me to pause when he could not keep up. His facial expression changed dramatically as God's Word began to penetrate his heart and mind.

I then pointed out that "All things work together for good to them that love God, to them who are the called according to His purpose" (Rom. 8:28). God wanted him to learn something from his situation and be thankful for what he had gone through (1 Thes. 5:18). He wondered how he could thank God, since the whole situation had been so terrible.

I suggested that he thank God (1) that he was coming out of the valley of despair, (2) that he had learned to apply biblical principles, and (3) that he could counsel with others similarly worried. God wants us to thank Him for our worrisome situations. In this way, we focus on what He wants to do with us rather than on ourselves and what we want to do.

Difference between Planning and Worrying. Some people seem so carefree, but their problem may be a lack of planning. Theirs is the spirit of the old saying "Whatever will be, will be." Both worry and lack of planning are wrong.

God does not want us to worry, but he does want us to plan. The Book of Proverbs has considerable teaching about planning. Also, James 4:13-15 instructs us to make plans, but to turn them over to God. Then if He wills, those plans will reach fruition.

I can plan for the future without worrying about it. But if I worry about the future and the implementation of my plans, then I am trying to rob God of the future because He only gives me one day at a time to live.

How to Conquer Worry. Two prerequisites for conquering worry are rest and recognition of God's timing. The psalmist wrote: "It is vain for you to rise up early, to sit up late, to eat the bread of sorrows: for so He giveth His beloved sleep" (Ps. 127:2). Lack of adequate sleep always increases our potential for worry. Consequently, I have found that a good night of rest helps to eliminate worry.

Second, God's timing is important. This is a good reminder for us, especially when we are in a hurry. One time I thought that surely a promotion was due me. I worried about it and why it had not come. When it finally came, I recognized that God had used this time to teach me about waiting for His timing.

Once these prerequisites have been met, if one is still worried, I make three suggestions: (1) define his problem, (2) pray about what God wants him to learn from the problem, and (3) pray about a solution to the problem. Often an attempt to thoroughly define a problem reveals that there really is no problem at all.

Never worry about the consequences of doing what God wants you to do. When God directed us to change churches because of errant doctrinal teaching, my wife worried about how our children would adapt. They immediately came to like the new church far better than the old, and my wife confessed one night how upset she had been at the prospect of changing churches—a change that God wanted.

Why should a Christian *ever* worry? Jesus is coming again. Some 1,845 times the Bible speaks of the second coming of Christ. Numerically, it is probably the most emphatic teaching of the New Testament. For example, Paul mentioned baptism 12 times, but the Second Coming 50 times. Why worry when we are told that the causes of earthly worry will be wiped out in eternity?

And God shall wipe away all tears from their eyes; and there shall be no more death, neither sorrow, nor crying, neither shall there be any more pain: for the former things are passed away (Rev. 21:4).

"See then that you walk circumspectly, not as fools, but as wise, redeeming the time, because the days are evil."

Ephesians 5:15-16

10

Time Managed

Long past midnight on a cold and snowy Saturday night, the telephone rang in my boyhood home. A friend was calling to say he was stuck in the snow with his date at Lake Bloomington, 14 miles to the north of my home. He wanted me to come and get them.

The need was urgent, but I told him, "No." Why?

First, it was not important that I go. He had not called his parents who could have gone, because he did not want them to know he was out so late with a date at such a forlorn place.

Second, I had only returned an hour or two before from a collegiate debating trip to Chicago and was very tired. I needed a good night of rest to be prepared to teach my Sunday School class of seventh-grade boys the next morning.

Third, on such a bad night, my going in a fatigued condition might have compounded the problem rather than remedying it. Besides, my friend needed to learn not to hide his wrongdoing from his parents.

Christians often jump at the chance to help another person because the need is urgent. But sometimes we fail to discern if the need is really *important*. We end up doing many good and urgent things, but we sacrifice more important matters. Being prepared for my seventh grade class was the important need for me.

As a professor living in Clemson, South Carolina, I was asked by an association of neighbors in our subdivision to serve as its president. Without adequately praying and discerning God's desire for me, I said "Yes" only to withdraw a few weeks later when it was apparent that I had made the wrong decision.

My initial decision was based on very good reasons. I was serving my neighbors, helping the community, and seemingly broadening my opportunities to witness. The chairman of the nominating committee said that my leadership experience was greatly needed and that he wanted to know my decision the next day.

When I later withdrew, it was because: (1) completion of a textbook manuscript demanded more time, (2) preparation for my college Sunday School class of 100 pupils necessitated more time, and (3) speaking at numerous churches also required more time. I had learned to establish my priorities.

In the case of the snowbound friend, I made the right decision initially, but in the second case, the wrong one. Both reflect problems we all face. But they both focus on our choice to use our time for the best purposes. In both cases, I was impressed by the urgency of taking action, but that would have resulted in neglecting the really important.

Scripturally, why should a Christian be concerned about time management? And how should a Christian manage time? These two fundamental questions separate effective Christians from ineffective.

Why Manage Time?

Life gives us time plus resources. In the simplest way of looking at life's possibilities, we have only two ingredients to mix successfully: our time and our resources. Resources include our abilities.

As a high school student, I received a booklet from my uncle who was an insurance salesman about how to sell insurance. In it was a quote I shall never forget: "The successful person forms the habit of doing what failures don't like to do." To be a successful Christian, we must develop the habit of managing our time and using our resources and abilities in a scriptural way.

There are at least seven scriptural reasons for time management. *Time is an investment that is to accrue divine dividends.* As Christians, we are to produce fruit for God. John recorded Jesus' words: "I have chosen you, and ordained you, that you should go and bring forth fruit, and that your fruit should remain" (John 15:16). Just as orange trees reproduce oranges, so Christians are to reproduce Christians. Just as an individual invests money to earn interest or dividends, so Christians are to invest their time to earn interest or dividends in the form of new Christians maturing in the faith. We are to produce not just fruit, but fruit that lasts. And that requires time well utilized. I cannot expect to win people to Christ unless I witness; neither can I expect these new converts to grow as Christians unless I train them. To accomplish these two biblical injunctions of witnessing and discipling, I must devote prime time.

We must be "redeeming the time" (Eph. 5:16). The word redeem here means "buying up the opportunity"—that is, to put to best use or to take maximum advantage of opportunities. Since the word *redeeming* is a present participle, it means to be continually or constantly turning each opportunity to best advantage. Thus, the Christian should always evaluate his life to make sure that he is actually redeeming the time.

A word of caution is in order here. Concern about redeeming the time should not lead us to worry about it. I have known people to be so worried about whether they were correctly using their time that regardless of what they did they used their time ineffectively.

Scripture teaches that we have limited time. Our lives are but as "vapor that appeareth for a little time, and then vanisheth away" (James 4:14). The longer I live the more I wish that I had made better use of my time from my late teens through early 30s. For example, if I had only memorized one more verse of Scripture per week during those years, I would know many additional Bible verses. And if I had witnessed to just one more person per week, many more people would have heard the Gospel. I was doing many other things during this time period, but not necessarily the best things. I was not efficiently using my spare time to witness and to memorize Scripture.

Christians have an obligation to set an example to others as to how they use their time. Paul expressed this reason for time management. "For yourselves know how you ought to follow us; for we behaved not ourselves disorderly among you; neither did we eat any man's bread for nought; but wrought with labor and travail night and day; that we might not be chargeable to any of you; not because we have not power, but to make ourselves an ensample unto you to follow us" (2 Thes. 3:7-9).

Paul outlined at least three key principles here of time management for the Christian: (1) offering or organizing our time, (2) working so as not to be beholden to anyone, and (3) being an example worthy of emulation.

Temptation and sin tend to enter much more easily during idle times than during active times. How much easier it is to gossip if I am engaging in idle chatter with no particular focus on my conversation! Jesus rebuked idle chatter. "But I say unto you, that every idle word that men shall speak, they shall give account thereof in the day of judgment. For by thy words thou shalt be justified, and by thy words thou shalt be condemned" (Matt. 12:36-37).

Paul also rebuked idleness and its common results, disorder and gossip: "For we hear that there are some which walk among you disorderly, working not at all, but are busybodies" (2 Thes. 3:11).

We answer for our time. A verse that has meant much to me is: "Rejoice, O young man, in thy youth; and let thy heart cheer thee in the days of thy youth, and walk in the ways of thine heart, and in the sight of thine eyes: but know thou, that for all these things God will bring thee into judgment" (Ecc. 11:9). Our use of time will be judged by God.

A Christian's life and his time are to be ordered by God. Paul wrote, "For we are His workmanship, created in Christ Jesus unto good works, which God hath before ordained that we should walk in them" (Eph. 2:10).

How to Manage Time

As I mentioned before, successful people make a habit of doing what others don't like to do. Effective time management is the development of godly habits based on scriptural principles. Seven habits important to time management are illustrated in two Old Testament case studies: Saul's refusal to wait on Samuel to offer the sacrifice and Jethro's counsel to Moses about delegating work.

Saul's sin of time mismanagement (1 Sam. 13:7-13).

As for Saul, he was yet in Gilgal, and all the people followed him trembling. And he tarried seven days, according to the set time that Samuel had appointed: but Samuel came not to Gilgal; and the people were scattered from him. And Saul said, "Bring hither a burnt offering to me, and peace offerings." And he offered the burnt offering. And it came to pass, that as soon as he had made an end of offering the burnt offering, behold, Samuel came; and Saul went out to meet him, that he might salute him. And Samuel said, "What hast thou done?" And Saul said, "Because I saw that the people were scattered from me, and that thou camest not within the days appointed, and that the Philistines gathered themselves together at Michmash; therefore said I, 'The Philistines will come down now upon me to Gilgal, and I have not made supplication unto the Lord:' I forced myself therefore, and offered a burnt offering." And Samuel said to Saul, "Thou hast done foolishly: thou hast not kept the commandment of the Lord thy God, which He commanded thee: for now would the Lord have established thy kingdom upon Israel for ever. But now thy kingdom shall not continue: the Lord hath sought him a man after His own heart, and the Lord hath commanded him to be captain over His people, because thou hast not kept that which the Lord commanded thee."

Moses' time management example (Ex. 18:13-26).

And it came to pass on the morrow, that Moses sat to judge the people: and the people stood by Moses from the morning unto the evening. And when Moses' father-in-law saw all that he did to the people, he said, "What is this thing that thou doest to the people? Why sittest thou thyself alone, and all the people stand by thee from morning unto even?" And Moses said unto his father-in-law, "Because the people come unto me to inquire of God: when they have a matter, they come unto me; and I judge between one and another, and I do make them know the statutes of God, and His laws." And Moses' father-in-law said unto him, "The thing that thou doest is not good. Thou wilt surely wear away, both thou, and this people that is with thee: for this thing is too heavy for thee; thou art not able to perform it thyself alone. Hearken now unto my voice, I will give thee counsel, and God shall be with thee: be thou for the people to God-ward, that thou mayest bring the causes unto God: and thou shalt teach them ordinances and laws, and shalt show them the way wherein they must walk, and the work that they must do. Moreover thou shalt provide out of all the people able men, such as fear God, men of truth, hating covetousness; and place such over them, to be rulers of thousands, and rulers of hundreds, rulers of fifties, and rulers of tens: and let them judge the people at all seasons: and it shall be, that every great matter they shall bring unto thee, but every small matter they shall judge: so shall it be easier for thyself, and they shall bear the burden with thee. If thou shalt do this thing, and God command thee so, then thou shalt be able to endure, and all this people shall also go to their place in peace." So Moses harkened to the voice of his father-in-law, and did all that he had said.

What are the habits that the successful person forms?

1. Inner direction. A Christian's time management should be determined by God's desires and demands, not those of the world. The habit of resisting the world's demands is often difficult to develop because it may mean waiting on God for a period of time. The demand on Saul was to unify the people and to prepare for battle against the Philistines. He wanted to seek God's pleasure by offering a sacrifice, which was a perfectly laudable objective if done at the right time in the right manner and by the right person. But Saul was the wrong person doing it in the wrong way at the wrong time. Saul's lack of inner direction is shown again in 1 Samuel 15:24: "And Saul said unto Samuel, 'I have sinned; for I have transgressed the commandment of the Lord, and thy words; because I feared the people, and obeyed their voice.' "

Little wonder God wanted another king. The habit of inner direction necessitates saying No, even to resist doing what may appear to be good. God doesn't want us to do every good thing, just the right and best.

Also, the habit of inner direction means letting those responsible for performing duties execute their work. Saul would not wait for Samuel to offer the sacrifice. Even today, leaders should teach responsibility by letting people do their assigned tasks and not interfering unless it is absolutely essential. Of course, Saul should not have performed Samuel's duties under any circumstance since God had directly delegated them to Samuel.

2. *Avoid the fire fighter syndrome.* Many people are like fire fighters, constantly rushing to put out a fire because that is the urgent need. Of course, that is what fire fighters are supposed to do, because the urgent and the important coincide in their work.

The fire fighter mentality among Christians arises from people being too busy—always on the run. If a Christian is constantly on the run, he should evaluate whether he is doing too much, or doing the wrong things, or doing things in the wrong way.

King Saul succumbed to the "fire fighter" syndrome when he responded to the urgent need to offer a sacrifice in preparation for war with the Philistines. Samuel was not there, so he rushed in to do the job. The tyranny of the urgent caused him to lose the tranquility that comes from doing the important. He was doing too much, doing the wrong thing, and doing it in the wrong way.

3. *Evaulation and introspection.* Notice that Saul immediately tried to justify and rationalize his actions to Samuel (1 Sam. 13:12). What God wants, however, are men humble enough to look at what they did, admit their mistakes, and then take

corrective action. Just suppose that Saul had been humble enough to do those things in this instance. He would have avoided the pattern of mismanagement of time which cost him his throne.

I once had a particularly demanding schedule as the administrative assistant to a U. S. Senator from New York. I had to reevaluate my use of time on a regular basis. Some days, I left the office with 25 telephone messages waiting to be returned and a stack of correspondence still to be answered. That was in addition to managing three offices and some 50 people. The leftover work alone was enough for more than one day. Yet the next day a similar amount of work was added. There was often no relief from the hectic pace. At times like these, we can apply Jethro's advice to Moses and develop three time-saving habits: seeking counsel from others, delegating the work, and learning to relax.

4. Seeking counsel. After I assumed the position as administrative assistant, I sought counsel from present and former administrative assistants to senators. From them I learned ways to do my work efficiently and effectively. Also, I consulted my subordinates in the office as well as the senator himself. I needed counsel from people outside and inside the office, as well as from my superiors and my subordinates in order to better understand how to organize my time.

5. Delegation of work. Jethro advised Moses to train subordinates and delegate work to them. In my example, if I had returned those calls and answered those letters, I would have had very little time for planning and administering the affairs of the three offices. Therefore, I trained other people to handle most of the telephone calls and correspondence.

This principle of delegation also works in a home. My wife and I assign specific chores to our children. In this way, they learn to perform their duties and to appreciate the importance of their responsibilities. For example, when I wash our cars, Charlie and Josh are given tasks such as scrubbing the white wall tires. I am always amazed at how well they work and at how much work they save me. Also, they get a thrill out of doing the work.

People who live with us or work for us like to have a sense of accomplishment which only comes by giving them responsibilities and allowing them to perform those functions generally free of our interference.

6. *Relaxation.* Certain large corporations emphasize that their executives have adequate time to relax. No doubt this was one reason for Jethro's counsel to Moses, who was overburdened with work. We need to avoid the "workaholic" syndrome by seeking a balance between work and relaxation. I do this by never taking work home. In this way, I can concentrate on family activities, house chores, and reading. Although I used to work nights and on Saturdays before we had children, I have tried to eliminate night and Saturday work altogether. As a result, my daytime work is much more efficient.

7. *Time efficiency.* Three principles are useful in learning to properly use your time. First, try to concentrate your work during your most efficient hours. My efficiency is much greater from 8 till 11 A.M., 1 till 3 P.M., and 6 till 9 P.M. So I try to schedule my most important duties for these hours. Evaluate your own cycle of efficiency to determine when you are most efficient. Then concentrate your work during those periods.

Second, try to use your spare moments to maximum advantage. For example, if I am attending a meeting that lapses into trivia, I always have Bible verse cards with me to begin reviewing.

Third, keep a daily schedule of tasks. I call mine my "attack sheet." It may contain both short- and long-range projects, and I don't try to work on each project every day. Rather, I use the attack sheet to set priorities for each day and for the future. The list helps me to distinguish the urgent from the less important by giving me an overview of the work to be done.

At the age of 12, Jesus said: "Wist you not that I must be about my Father's business?" (Luke 2:49). Then in the twilight of His life at the age of 33, He reported to the Father: "I have glorified Thee on earth; I have finished the work which Thou gavest Me to do" (John 17:4). Jesus' time was well managed. The whole of John 17 is, in many respects, a report to the Father on Jesus' management of His time. In the same way, we must ultimately answer to God for how our time is managed.

"Thou wilt keep him in perfect peace, whose mind is stayed on Thee; because he trusteth in Thee."

Isaiah 26:3

11

How to Defend Jesus Christ

Suppose you were delivering your last lecture or speaking to the last group of people you would ever have an opportunity to address, what would you say?

When I was a graduate student, distinguished professors from all disciplines on our campus were asked to deliver their "last lecture" in the university-wide Last Lecture Series. Frequently I probed the dilemma which must have faced those professors as they wrestled with the nature of their enduring legacy to others.

Would I, for example, lecture on a subject narrowly related to my own discipline of political science? Or possibly on a subject which speaks broadly to the critical issues of our day? Would I attempt an inspirational lecture on climbing every mountain and facing every problem? What would be most important for me to communicate?

I was teaching at the University of Illinois during the throes of radical-revolutionary ferment. As I approached the end of the semester, I wondered what could be imparted to students at a time of division and dissension. The 50 students in my class had a diversity of backgrounds, representing broadly the spectra of philosophical, political, ideological, and theological points of view—from the extreme left to the extreme right, and including Protestants, Catholics, and Jews.

Our course, titled the American Presidency, had been significant enough, but during those trying times I felt deeply the obligation to leave with those students something more than provocative lectures and stimulating books about the American Presidency. During those days of confusion and consternation, I wanted to leave them something no professor or teacher of mine had ever left with me: the meaning I found in life.

As I began the last few minutes of that last class of the semester, you could have heard a pin drop. Both the radical revolutionaries and the staid conservatives listened with rapt attention. What a privileged experience to simply tell what I believe to students, many of whom had only recently participated in shutting down the University of Illinois, a campus of over 30,000 students.

The reactions of three students were revealing. If you had to pick just one radical revolutionary in the class, Michael would have been that student. During the semester, whenever I would say anything the least bit bordering on radical thought, Michael could be seen almost rising up out of his chair to cheer me on. Stopping by to see me a few days after that last class, he said: "Professor, I just want you to know it took guts to say what you said the last few minutes of that last class period. I've never had a professor or a teacher ever before tell me what was on the inside of him. Every professor ought to be required to tell his students what makes him tick. Next time, don't wait until the last few minutes of the last class period. Start out the first few minutes of the first class!"

And then the reactions of two brilliant Jewish students were important. Mr. H and Miss A, rather than being offended by my convictions which differed from theirs, became my closest friends among those students. I think it was because they recognized I was honestly relating my personal philosophy of life. That philosophy would be the content of my last lecture.

The Purpose of Life

The search for meaning in life cannot be denied. Mark Twain once said: "From the cradle to his grave a man never does a single thing which has any first and foremost object save one—to secure peace of mind—spiritual comfort for himself." Mark Twain did not share my personal philosophy of life, but he did identify what most people in one way or another identify as their goal in life, namely, peace of mind.

Whether through a drug cult or consciousness-raising group, whether through psychiatry, or through a guru, people from all walks of life are searching for meaning in life—inner happiness and peace of mind. Certain truths have given me meaning in life. They may not persuade you that I am right and you are wrong, but I give them simply in the spirit of intellectual honesty.

Even though we do not live in the tumult of revolutionary currents today, scholars are deeply concerned about the future of the American civilization. A cursory reading of Gibbon's *Rise and Fall of the Roman Empire* and Arnold Toynbee's *A Study of History* readily establishes many frightening parallels between our civilization and the other great civilizations which plunged to ruin. Herbert Spencer's analogy that civilizations have four seasons, spring, summer, fall, and winter suggests that the winter of our civilization may be at hand.

One of Shakespeare's three witches in *Macbeth* aptly described the climate of our day when she said: "Fair is foul and foul is fair, hovers through the fog and filthy air." Each day's news seems to bring new reality to what would seem the impossible and unbelievable. A well-respected member of the United States Senate, William Proxmire (D.—Wis.), stated in a nonpolitical comment: "As a people we are a physical wreck. We are too fat, too soft, too tense. We are prone to alcoholism and increasingly to drug addiction. We are lazy. We are thoughtfully self-indulgent and unless we straighten out, we are not long for leadership."

Indeed, it is now difficult to hold to Charles Dickens' fleeting line of hope that these are the best of times and worst of times. Increasingly they seem like only the worst of times.

We live in an age of discontinuity where our existence appears to float amidst a meaningless mosaic of fragments.

Many of the great minds in history have recognized that "the past is but prologue," which is to say that we cannot adequately analyze the present nor explore the future without a firm understanding of the past. In *The Gothic Chamber*, Goethe stated the importance of historical understanding:

> Who can think of something stupid,
> Who can think of something smart
> That prior ages haven't thought of?

I turn back the pages of history in order to see what great minds have said about my philosophy of life. Specifically, I would like to test it against its intellectual antagonists and scholarly critics.

Man or Myth

This philosophy of life intently focuses on a Person about whom more has been written than any other. *The Encyclopedia Britannica* has devoted more words, approximately 20,000 in all, to Him, than to any other person. And the 10 volumes of Toynbee's *A Study of History* give comparable treatment.

Is this Person, Jesus Christ, man or myth, hoax or history? What really has been the value of His impact on history?

Antagonists and scholars in many walks of life during many periods of history and from many vantage points quickly give us the answer to our first question.

From England, contemporary University of Manchester theology professor F. F. Bruce says:

> Some writers may toy with the fancy of a 'Christ-myth,' but they do not do so on the ground of historical evidence. The historicity of Christ is as axiomatic for an unbiased historian as the historicity of Julius Caesar. It is not the historians who propagate the 'Christ-myth' theories.

The *New York Times* reported on the first page of the February 13, 1972, edition that two Hebrew University archeologists had discovered an Arabic manuscript of the Jewish historian Josephus which authentically documented the historical evidence of Jesus. The archeologists who discovered the manuscript are Jews; the historian is a Jew never associated with the Christian faith; the manuscript is Arabic.

Another Jewish historian, David Strauss, has said Jesus Christ "is historical, not mythical; is an individual, no mere symbol . . ."

Harvard University professor Clifford Herschel Moore stated that the Christian faith "was founded on positive, historical, and acceptable facts."

University of London professor emeritus, recipient of the Faraday medal and honorary fellow of St. John's College, Cambridge, Ambrose Fleming concluded that the Christian philosophy of life "is not founded on fictions, or nourished on delusions, or . . . 'cunningly devised fables,' but on historical and actual events, which, however strange they may be, are indeed the greatest events which ever happened in the world."

Before writing the novel *Ben Hur*, Lew Wallace devoted some two years of study to establish the myth of Jesus Christ. As a result of his studies, Lew Wallace became a Christian.

The evidence on the actual existence of Jesus Christ is not only abundant, but overwhelming. His existence cannot be denied. He is not myth.

Impact on History

And now the second and in some respects more important question: What has been the value of His impact on history? Flowing from the pens of unbiased scholars is a flood of ink indelibly inscribing the virtues of Jesus Christ.

One of the great thinkers and writers from the Unitarian tradition, William E. Channing, eloquently stated:

The sages and heroes of history are receding from us, and history contracts the records of the deeds into a narrower and narrower page. But time has no power over the name and deeds and words of Jesus Christ.

Yale University historian Kenneth Scott Latourette has noted:

It is evidence of His (Jesus') importance, of the effect that He has had upon history and presumably, of the baffling mystery of His being that no other life ever lived on this planet has evoked so huge a volume of literature among so many peoples and languages, and that, far from ebbing, the flood continues to mount.

On *perfection*, Ralph Waldo Emerson said: "Jesus is the most perfect of all men that have yet appeared."

On the *universality of His importance*, the Unitarian preacher Theodore Parker said that Jesus Christ "rises free from all prejudices of his age, nation, or sect . . ."

On *greatness*, Islam's *Koran* concludes that Jesus Christ is ". . . the greatest above all in this world and in the world to come."

On *personality*, Jewish novelist Sholom Asch says, "Jesus Christ is the outstanding personality of all time."

On *symbolic value*, historian Thomas Carlyle indicates Jesus Christ is ". . . our divinest symbol. Higher has the human thought not yet reached."

On *a model for life*, three great minds, none of whom claimed to be Christian, made these comments.

Johann Wolfgang von Goethe stated that "the human mind, no matter how far it may advance in every other department, will never transcend the height and moral culture of Christianity as it shines and glows in the Gospels."

Jean Jacques Rousseau, a political philosopher, said: "When Plato describes his imaginary righteous man, loaded with all the punishments of guilt, yet meriting the highest rewards of virtue, he describes exactly the character of Jesus."

And John Stuart Mill, another political philosopher, stated it would be difficult for a non-Christian "to find a better translation of the rule of virtue from the abstract into the concrete than to endeavor to live so that Christ would approve of . . . (one's) life."

On the *perfection of human culture*, the German scientist and philosopher, Ernst Haeckel, a protagonist of atheistic rationalism, concluded: "Beyond all doubt the present degree of human culture owes, in great part, its perfection to the propagation of the Christian system of morals and its ennobling influence."

Also on the perfection of human culture, William Lecky, a

historian from England, concludes as did Haeckel: "The simple record of (Jesus Christ's) . . . three short years of active life has done more to regenerate and soften mankind than all the disquisitions of philosophers and moralists."

And finally, on the *acquisition of knowledge*, George Bancroft states that "Christianity has attracted to itself the profoundest thinkers of the human race, and is in no way hindered by the ever-advancing tide of human knowledge."

Countering Criticism

Tributes from intellectuals and critics could go on and on. But let us stop here to examine two critical charges against this philosophy of life.

First, the charges made by Aldous Huxley and Bertrand Russell, both agnostics if not atheists. Second, the charge that much evil has been done in the name of this philosophy of life.

Concerning Huxley and Russell, one must examine the premises of their charges. For example, Huxley stated that he "had motives for not wanting the world to have meaning." And with Russell, scholars are doubtful if he carefully examined the four Gospels, the original source of the Christian philosophy of life, when he wrote the book entitled *Why I Am Not a Christian*. So we must ask:

Do we want to accept the charges of one who claimed that he did not want life to have meaning?

Do we want to accept the charges of another who misunderstood the philosophy that he criticized?

Concerning the charge that much evil has been done in the name of Christianity, we would be blind to the facts of history not to acknowledge its legitimacy. So how do I respond?

The same charge could be made about other things. Most of us would quickly concede that any one of our favorite sports—football, baseball, or basketball—is good, but we would also have to agree that sports can be used for evil purposes, such as gamblers getting players to engage in point-shaving scandals. Whenever one finds something good, it will not be uncommon to find persons with sinister motives ready to take advantage of the good in order to achieve wrongful ends.

So it is with Christianity. Wars have been fought and cultural practices defended which bear no resemblance to the tenets of Jesus Christ's teachings in the Gospels.

A friend of mine clearly distinguishes between cultural religion and biblical faith. He says, "Much of the organized church of today . . . has allowed its thinking and its values to be conformed to the world. In subtle ways we allow our culture with its civil religion to determine our relationship to political power instead of the Scriptures and the revelation of Christ."

Certainly, if all I knew about the Christian philosophy of life were some of our culture's misrepresentations of that philosophy, I too would reject it. Fortunately, my philosophy of life is deeply personal, requiring a commitment of myself to Jesus Christ and not a justification or rationalization of cultural misrepresentations of Jesus Christ's life.

The Crucible of Life

According to the teaching of Jesus Christ, real meaning in life—inner happiness and peace of mind—comes through personal acceptance of Jesus Christ as one's sovereign ruler, or in His words, one's Lord and Saviour.

Jesus made several claims in essentially the same way on several occasions. He said:

I and the Father are one.

I have come that you might have an abundant life.

My peace I leave with you.

He who believes in Me has abundant life.

I am the Way, the Truth, and the Life.

In essence, He said, "I am God and as God I am the author of the only ultimate peace and meaning in life." He taught that the ultimate issue in life is whether a person accepts or rejects Him.

Those are fantastic claims for a man to make, and difficult claims for the intellectual to accept.

Fantastic claims, because they are either wondrously true or false. If true, then He is the divine Son of God. If false, the claims were made by a deluded person or history's greatest imposter.

Difficult claims, because they require denial of self, the deepest commitment for a self-sufficient intellectual to make. Let's look at how two intellectuals responded to these claims. First, C. S. Lewis, an antagonist and critic turned believer. Second, H. G. Wells, an antagonist and critic to the end. Both are among the great minds in the modern history of England.

C. S. Lewis, popular professor at both Oxford and Cambridge Universities, had students standing in the hallways outside his classroom to be within the sound of his voice. This proficient professor and prolific writer grappled with Jesus' fantastic claims on his journey from agnosticism to a personal commitment to Christ. He concluded that:

A man who was merely a man and said the sort of things Jesus said would not be a great moral teacher. He would either be a lunatic—on a level with the man who says he is a poached egg—or else he would be the Devil of hell. You must make your choice. Either this man was, and is, the Son of God, or else a madman or something worse. You can shut Him up for a fool, you can spit at Him and kill Him as a demon; or you can fall at His feet and call Him Lord and God. But let us not come up with any patronizing nonsense about His being a great human teacher. He has not left that open to us (*Mere Christianity*, 1943, MacMillan, p. 56).

Concerning H. G. Wells, a recent *New York Times* book review by Michael Holroyd of a Wells' biography says that this brilliant writer, ". . . despite all his ability and charm, was finally to waste . . . (his life)." One of Wells' terminal comments indicates the pessimism and lack of meaning he had in life. "This world is at the end of its tether . . . the end of everything we call life is close at hand and cannot be evaded."

While a student at Oxford, a friend of mine studied the life of H. G. Wells, and in this study he encountered a Wells' quotation which reveals why Wells thought he had not found meaning in life. On the occasion of his 71st birthday, Wells had gathered around him friends from around the world to whom he remarked: "Gentlemen, I am now 71 years old, and I've never found peace. The trouble with the likes of me is that the man from Galilee, Jesus of Nazareth, was too big for my small heart."

C. S. Lewis and H. G. Wells, both great minds. The one found meaning in life. The other did not.

Summarizing what Lewis accepted and Wells rejected, the distinguished Harvard University psychologist, Gordon W. Allport, says the Christian philosophy of life

. . . has everything. For the *theoretical mind* it can accommodate all that science can discover and still challenge science to dig deeper and deeper. For the *social mind* it contains the high-road to all successful and just social relations . . . For the *aesthetic mind* it gives an absolutely satisfying conception of harmony and beauty. For *economic and political minds*, it gives a meaning to production and power, and a guide to conduct . . .

. . . its goals and ideals are always ahead of what any human being can fully achieve . . . Christian objectives are too high to make complete achievement possible. Having once experienced the blessedness of certitude, though but for a moment, you will never be satisfied but will be impelled to seek to regain and extend this experience all your life long.

The preeminent challenge in life, according to Mark Twain, is to secure "peace of mind."

The purpose of this, my "last lecture," would be to test my philosophy of life, that which has given me peace of mind, against the comments of antagonists and critics. These intellectual giants provide convincing evidence for the authenticity of Jesus Christ and compelling testimony for the beneficent impact which His life has had upon history.

As one whose philosophy of life is based upon the surrender of my life to Jesus Christ, I can say He has given me meaning in life—inner happiness and peace of mind.

"The words of the Lord are pure words; as silver tried in a furnace of the earth, purified seven times."

Psalm 12:6

12

The Last Word

What is the foundation of your life? Do you have a foundation that will allow you to impart something of lasting value to others? The only foundation many people have is the current vogue of society. When it changes, they shift to another passing fad.

David Riesman, Harvard University sociologist, suggests in *The Lonely Crowd* that among types of people there are "other-directed" and "inner-directed" persons. The "other-directed" person depends upon what others say for what he does. The "inner-directed" person responds to internal convictions and standards.

If we depend upon what others say or think, then we surely have no solid foundation. The trend and fancy of public opinion changes about as quickly as modern fashions.

Some "inner-directed" persons, including outstanding intellectuals, have come to reject the foundation of their lives. Among them is the esteemed author and playwright George Bernard Shaw, who said:

The science to which I pinned my faith is bankrupt. . . . Its counsels which should have established the millenium have led directly to the suicide of Europe. I believed them once. . . . In their name, I helped destroy the faith of millions of worshipers in the temples of a million creeds. And now they look at me and witness the great tragedy of an atheist who has lost his faith.

What would you be able to tell others that is of lasting value? Will your life offer to others enduring substance after which they may model their lives? Or will those who come after you scorn the foundation of your life as mere shifting sand?

The central issue of life is one's foundation. That is, how you determine what is right and wrong, good and bad. What are your values, ethics, and standards of life? What provides order and meaning? Life's foundation is that which is most fundamental and basic to you. The superstructure of life, such as one's career, aspirations, and achievements, is built upon the foundation. If the foundation is unstable, the superstructure will tumble.

The foundation of American society and, indeed, the whole of Western civilization appears to be decaying rapidly. Rhodes Scholar and former American ambassador Murat W. Williams wrote in The Chronicle of Higher Education about the importance of truthfulness. He traces that quality in America's past to the influence of the Bible.

A brilliant and influential graduate of a great church university told me the other day that he did not know the Ananias story. "Who," he asked, "was Ananias?"

My eyes opened wider. I could see that the lie had really lost its horror. In earlier times, pious Americans warned the young that if they lied, they would meet the fate of Ananias. . . . Laxity about lying quickens the pace of the spreading corruption of our society. To professionalize lying guarantees our decline.

It will go on like that until we restore the lost deterrent which we had in the Ananias story . . . Compromised honor systems, unpunished offenses, suspended sentences, and lavish rewards do not add up to a credible deterrent.

The foundation for my living, the Bible, has been bombarded with derogatory attacks throughout history. To make sure I am on solid ground, I need to test my foundation for living against the arguments raised by its detractors. If it passes this test, it will offer a solid, unique foundation for you to consider.

These are the questions I must answer:

Has the Bible had a beneficial impact on society?
Is the Bible truly the word of God?
Does the Bible contain errors?

Contributions to History

Although the Bible's contributions to history merit more space than is available in this chapter, we can still outline some of the scope of the Bible's contributions to society.

On its contributions to literature. Biblical allusions dot the horizons of classical literature with: over 400 in Tennyson's works; over 600 in Browning's works; some 700 in Shakespeare's works; and literally thousands in Milton's works.

On its continuing influence. The French atheist Voltaire predicted the Bible's extinction in 100 years. At the end of that 100-year period, Voltaire's own home was owned and used by the Geneva Bible Society, and the Bible continued to be the world's best-seller.

On Israel's survival as a nation. David Ben Gurion said: "It is the Bible that has kept us alive all these centuries, and it is the Bible that holds the greatest hope for our survival in the future."

On the foundation of American public schools. Former U.S. Supreme Court Justice William O. Douglas says: "Our American public school system goes back to November 11, 1647, when Massachusetts provided that every town having 100 or more families or households should have a grammar school supported by the taxpayers. The preamble of the law referred to that 'auld deluder Satan' who tries to keep man from knowledge of the Scriptures, and it stated that the purpose of training children is so they may know the Word first-hand and not be deceived by those who put 'false glosses' on it."

On the power to change a life. Helen Keller said: "Somehow the mystery of language was revealed to me. I learned, for instance, that the word 'water' meant that wonderful cool something that flowed over my hand. Now I know the living Word—God's Word—awakened my soul, gave it light, hope, joy and set me free."

On help in the crises of life. Captain Eddie Rickenbacker declared: "I probably would not be here today if it had not been for the spiritual light and the moral power derived from the Bible. It has carried me through many crises of life."

Is there any book that has had a greater impact on mankind than the Bible? Can its beneficent contributions be denied? Is there any book that has ever sold more copies? Is there any book available in more languages?

What book inspired men and women to risk their lives to take medical and other scientific advances to the heartlands of Africa, China, and India?

What book inspired the founding of Harvard, Yale, Princeton, and a host of the nation's best colleges and universities?

What book inspired William Wilberforce to lead the fight against slavery in England?

What book led British Prime Minister Gladstone to fight for the underprivileged?

What book contains the teaching that liberated women from their suppressed state in the first century, A.D.?

What book inspired and continues to provide the basis for helping derelicts in skid-row missions of all the nation's major cities?

We could dwell much longer on the Bible's beneficent impact on history. But that is the easiest question of the three to answer. The next two related questions will be considered together: Is the Bible the Word of God? and, Is it truth without any mixture of error?

The defense of the Bible as God's unerring Word rests upon (1) the claims of a variety of people and a diversity of evidence, (2) the credibility of those who question these claims, (3) the consistency of logic, and (4) the consequences of unbelief in the claims.

Claims

Winston Churchill said of the Bible's truthfulness as the very Word of God:

We may be sure that all these things happened just as they are set out according to Holy Writ. We may believe that they happened to people not so very different from ourselves, and that the impressions those people received were faithfully recorded and have been transmitted across the centuries with far more accuracy than many of the telegraphed accounts we read of the goings-on of today. In the words of a forgotten work of Mr. Gladstone, we rest with assurance upon "The impregnable Rock of Holy Scripture."

Claims of Jesus Christ. Jesus Christ never questioned Scripture on historic, scientific, or spiritual grounds. Even the critics concede this point. Harvard University professor H. J. Cadbury, a critic of biblical infallibility, said that Jesus was more certain of the infallibility of the Old Testament than He was of His own messiahship.

The Bible's leading "demythologizer," Rudolph Bultmann, said that "Jesus always agreed with the scribes of His time in accepting without question the authority of the (Old Testament) Law."

The church's leading historian of modern times, Adolph Harnack, said Jesus was in agreement with His apostles, the Jews, and the entire early church that the Bible is free of error.

Of course, we should not merely accept the secondhand testimony of critics. We should also examine the very words of Jesus.

In many ways and on many occasions, Jesus attested to an inerrant and infallible Scripture. Never once did He question any portion of Old Testament Scripture, including the story of Jonah. Indeed, He said:

"The Scripture cannot be broken" (John 10:35).

"One jot or one tittle [the smallest elements of the alphabet of Jesus' day] shall in no wise pass from the law, till all be fulfilled" (Matt. 5:18).

"Heaven and earth shall pass away, but My words shall not pass away" (Mark 13:31).

Jesus placed such emphasis on the authority of Scripture that He said:

"Whosoever therefore shall be ashamed of Me and of My words . . . of him also shall the Son of man be ashamed when He cometh in the glory of His Father with the holy angels" (Mark 8:38).

"He that rejecteth Me and receiveth not My words hath one that judgeth him; the word that I have spoken, the same shall judge him in the last day" (John 12:48).

Evidently, one who rejects the words of Jesus about Scripture places himself in a very precarious position. In effect, he rejects what Jesus accepted and thereby claims that he knows more than Jesus. If Jesus is the Son of God as He says He is, can anyone know more than He knows?

Claims of the Bible. Note what the Bible says about itself. On this question, a Bible scholar from New York's Union Theological Seminary, F. C. Grant, declared: "Everywhere (in the Bible) it is taken for granted that what is written in Scripture is the work of divine inspiration, and is therefore trustworthy, infallible, and inerrant."

This is, of course, what Scripture says. Nearly 4,000 times the Old Testament claims to be transmitting the very words of God. The same claim is also scattered throughout the New Testament.

More poignantly and dramatically, the psalmist said, "The words of the Lord are pure words: as silver tried in a furnace of the earth, purified seven times" (Ps. 12:6). Among the ways the Bible refers to itself are:

"the Scripture . . . of God" (2 Tim. 3:16).

"the voice of His Word" (Ps. 103:20).

"the lively oracles of God" (Acts 7:38; Rom. 3:2).

"the Word of God" (Mark 7:13).

Claims of Christian leaders. We should also examine claims of the Christians, beginning with the first century fathers. The historic flow of evidence for nearly 20 centuries from the pens of church fathers weighs overwhelmingly, if not uniformly, on the side of an inerrant and an infallible Bible.

In the first century, Polycarp, a student of John the Apostle, concluded that the Scriptures are "the very voice of the Most

High" and that anyone who distorts them is "the first-born of Satan."

In the fifth century, Augustine wrote, "The faith will totter if the authority of the Holy Scriptures loses its hold on men. We must surrender ourselves to the authority of Holy Scripture, for it can neither mislead nor be misled."

In the 16th century, Martin Luther considered scriptural contradiction an impossibility and that those advocating such are "senseless and obstinate hypocrites." He added:

If I profess with the loudest voice and clearest exposition every portion of the truth of God except precisely that little point which the world and the devil are at that moment attacking, I am not professing Christ. Where the battle rages there the loyalty of the soldier is proved and to be steady on all battle fronts besides, is mere flight and disgrace if he flinches at that point.

Also in the 16th century, John Calvin concluded that the Bible must be given "the same reverence which we owe to God, because it has proceeded from Him alone and has nothing human mixed in . . ."

In the 19th century, Charles H. Spurgeon held that "this is the book untainted by any error, but is pure, unalloyed, perfect truth. Why? Because God wrote it."

Twentieth-century theologian Arthur Pink wrote: "If the Bible is not inspired in the strictest sense of the Word, then it is worthless, for it claims to be God's Word."

The names and statements of a host of other church leaders could be added to this array of testimony, including John Wesley and the Roman Catholic Church fathers. At this juncture, however, we do well to listen to Josephus, the eminent non-Christian historian of the first century, who said: "There is no discrepancy in the facts recorded. They learnt their message by reason of the inspiration which they received from God. They compiled accurately the history of their own time."

Claims of Archeology. There remains yet another area of evidence to be examined—archeology. No archeological find has ever contradicted Scripture regardless of whether the archeologist was Christian or non-Christian. Associated Press Religion writer, George W. Cornell, says: "A swelling tide of discoveries through archeological and historical research have confirmed more and more of that ancient book—the Bible."

Yale University archeologist Millar Burrows contends: "The excessive skepticism of many liberal theologians stems not from a careful evaluation of the available data, but from an enormous predisposition against the supernatural."

The director and principal librarian of the British Museum, Sir Frederick Kenyon, stated that "the Christian can take the whole Bible in his hand and say without fear or hesitation that he holds in it the true Word of God, handed down without essential loss from generation to generation throughout the centuries."

Claims of Prophecy. Prophecy is a subject of much interest these days as illustrated by the provocative film and book, *The Late Great Planet Earth.* This subject merits more treatment than space affords here, but consider two facts about biblical prophecy.

First, fully 33 biblical prophecies concerning Jesus Christ have been fulfilled. Statisticians have calculated the odds of those same prophecies being fulfilled in the life of any individual living or dead, and those odds are one in 83 billion!

Second, what other book predicted with such uncanny accuracy the plight of the Jewish people, their dispersion from and return to the land of their ancestors?

Contesting the Critics' Credibility

It is important to ask a few questions about the Bible critics. Who are they? Where did they come from? What authority do they have to question the Bible?

C.S. Lewis wrote extensively and compellingly on the reality of the biblical message.

On the subversion of belief in an inerrant Bible, C.S. Lewis stated:

The undermining of the old orthodoxy (biblical authority) has been mainly the work of divines engaged in New Testament criticism. The authority of experts in that discipline is the authority in deference to whom we are asked to give up a huge mass of beliefs shared in common by the Early Church, the fathers, the Middle Ages, the Reformers, and even in the nineteenth century.

On skepticism about the credibility of these primarily 20th century critics, Lewis said:

I want to explain what it is that makes me skeptical about this authority. . . . First, whatever these men may be as biblical critics, I distrust them as critics. They seem to me to lack literary judgment, to be imperceptive about the very quality of the texts they are reading. . . . These men ask me to believe they can read between the lines of the old texts; the evidence is their obvious inability to read (in any sense worth discussing) the lines themselves. They claim to see fern-seed and can't see an elephant 10 yards away in broad daylight.

On the critics' critiques of his own writing, Lewis notes: My own impression is that in the whole body of my experience not one of these guesses has on any point been right; that the method (literary criticism) shows a record of 100 percent failure.

On the prince of biblical demythologizers, Rudolph Bultmann, Lewis questioned his ability and authority.

Dr. Bultmann never wrote a gospel. Has the experience of his learned, specialized, and no doubt meritorious life really given him any power of seeing into the minds of those long dead men who were caught up into what, on any view, must be regarded as the central religious experience of the whole human race?

On miracles in the Bible, Lewis charged the critics with insufficient criticism of their own age.

If one is speaking of authority, the united authority of all the biblical critics in the world counts here for nothing. On this they speak simply as men; men who are obviously influenced by, and perhaps insufficiently critical of, the spirit of the age they grew up in.

Finally, on the irresponsibility of biblical criticism, Lewis cast an ominous warning.

Remember, the biblical critics, whatever reconstructions they devise, can never be crudely proved wrong. Saint Mark is dead. When they meet Saint Peter there will be more pressing matters to discuss.

Consistency of Logic

I wonder if biblical critics have examined the overwhelming logical problems they have to resolve concerning Jesus, God, and the Bible itself. Ponder for a moment these questions of logic.

1. If Jesus taught that the Bible is free of all error, but knew that it was not, is He not guilty of deception?

2. If Jesus did not know that the Bible contains false statements, then can He be considered the omniscient Son of God?

3. Can God be pure and holy if the Book He has given us contains impurity?

4. Can God really be sovereign if He cannot give us through humans a Book free of error?

5. Can you trust Christ without trusting His Word?

6. If parts of the Bible are false, who decides what is true and what is false, and does not that person become the judge of God and His Word?

7. If God can intervene in space and time to give us spiritual truth in the Bible, why cannot He also give us historical and scientific truth in the same Book?

Consequences of Unbelief

I am glad that the burden of those logical problems does not fall on me. We need to confront the question: "Do biblical critics risk more than poor logic in undermining faith in an inerrant and infallible Bible?" The Bible says they do.

Proverbs 30:5-6 reads: "Every word of God is pure; He is a shield unto them that put their trust in Him. Add thou not unto

His words, lest He reprove thee, and thou be found a liar."

Deuteronomy 12:32 reads: "What thing soever I command you, observe to do it; thou shalt not add thereto, nor diminish from it."

Deuteronomy 4:2 reads: "You shall not add unto the word which I command you, neither shall you diminish aught from it, that you may keep the commandments of the Lord your God which I command you."

Revelation 22:18-19 reads: "For I testify unto every man that heareth the words of the prophecy of this Book, if any man shall add unto these things, God shall add unto him the plagues that are written in this Book; and if any man shall take away from the words of the Book of this prophecy, God shall take away his part out of the Book of Life, and out of the holy city, and from the things which are written in this Book."

I cannot compel anyone to believe these Scriptures. But in honestly considering the evidence, I would ask you to compare the last words of two scoffers of Christianity with those of an apostle of faith. The foes: W. Somerset Maugham and Robert Ingersoll; the apostle is Paul. Their comments were all made during the twilight of life. They were, shall we say, "last lectures." Which will be the model for your life philosophy?

W. Somerset Maugham reflected: "When I look back on my life . . . it seems to me strangely lacking in reality. . . . It may be that my heart, having found rest nowhere, had some deep ancestral craving for God and immortality which my reason would have no truck with."

Robert Ingersoll concluded: "Death is a narrow vale between the cold and barren peaks of two eternities. We cry aloud and the only answer is the wailing echo of our cry."

Paul rejoiced: "For I am now ready to be offered, and the time of my departure is at hand. I have fought a good fight . . . I have kept the faith. Henceforth there is laid up for me a crown of righteousness, which the Lord, the righteous judge, shall give to me at that day: and not to me only, but unto all them that love His appearing" (2 Tim. 4:6-8).